What's the Matter with Preaching Today?

Mike Graves

editor

Westminster John Knox Press

LOUISVILLE • LONDON

Book design by Sharon Adams
Cover design by Lisa Buckley

First edition
Published by Westminster John Knox Press
Louisville, Kentucky

This book is printed on acid-free paper that meets the American National Standards Institute Z39.48 standard. ⊚

PRINTED IN THE UNITED STATES OF AMERICA

04 05 06 07 08 09 10 11 12 13—10 9 8 7 6 5 4 3 2 1

Library of Congress Cataloging-in-Publication Data

What's the matter with preaching today? / edited by Mike Graves.—1st ed.
    p. cm.
  Includes bibliographical references.
  ISBN 0-664-22632-9 (alk. paper)
  1. Preaching.   I. Graves, Mike.

  BV4207.W46 2004
  251—dc22   2004041906

For Carol,
who knows what's the matter
and still loves me!

Contents

Acknowledgments

At the birthing of this book it now gives me great pleasure to look back on its conception. From 1989 (the year I first started to teach preaching) to the present, I have always required my students to read Harry Emerson Fosdick's essay, "What Is the Matter with Preaching?" Most of them are duly impressed, even more so when they realize the year in which it was published, 1928. Back in the late 1990s, as the seventy-fifth year of the essay's life approached, I wondered if something shouldn't be done to mark the occasion—an article, perhaps. I had not thought about a book at that point.

Then, in December of 2000, at the annual meeting of the Academy of Homiletics, I had the good fortune of meeting Stephanie Egnotovich of Westminster John Knox Press. She suggested it might actually make for a good book, a collection of essays on the subject all these years later. Since then, we have worked together to create this present volume, brainstorming on contributors and the focus of this collection. I am grateful for her persistence, patience, and editorial eye, as well as her pastoral ear.

I am also grateful for the contributors with whom I have had conversation and the joy of reading their works. Many of them are persons whose books I devoured long before I had the pleasure of knowing them personally. In particular, early conversations with Gardner Taylor, James Forbes, and William Sloane Coffin, all of whom had hoped to participate, were especially gratifying. I, along with many readers, can only imagine what they might have offered.

At the birthing of this book I am also grateful for the labor, now that it is over. Thanks are due to my colleagues at Central Baptist Theological

Seminary who offered support along the way, especially David May and Molly Marshall. More than anything I am grateful for my wife, Carol, and our three children, Michael, Melissa, and Michelle. What gifts you are in my life!

Contributors

David L. Bartlett is Lantz Professor of Preaching and Dean of Academic Affairs, Yale University Divinity School, New Haven, Connecticut.

David Buttrick is Drucilla Moore Buffington Professor Emeritus of Homiletics and Liturgics, The Divinity School, Vanderbilt University, Nashville, Tennessee.

Ernest T. Campbell was Preaching Minister, Riverside Church, New York City, 1968 to 1976; Professor of Preaching and Worship, Garrett-Evangelical Theological Seminary, Evanston, Illinois, 1980 to 1990.

Fred B. Craddock is Bandy Professor Emeritus of Preaching and New Testament, Candler School of Theology, Emory University, Atlanta, Georgia.

Marva J. Dawn is Teaching Fellow in Spiritual Theology at Regent College, Vancouver, British Columbia; and theologian/educator/author with "Christians Equipped for Ministry" in Vancouver, Washington.

Anna Carter Florence is Assistant Professor of Preaching, Columbia Theological Seminary, Decatur, Georgia.

Mike Graves is Professor of Homiletics and Worship, Central Baptist Theological Seminary, Kansas City, Kansas; and Regional Minister of Preaching for the Greater Kansas City Christian Church (Disciples of Christ).

Cleophus J. LaRue is Francis Landey Patton Associate Professor of Homiletics, Princeton Theological Seminary, Princeton, New Jersey.

Thomas G. Long is Bandy Professor of Preaching, Candler School of Theology, Emory University, Atlanta, Georgia.

Eugene L. Lowry is William K. McElaney Professor Emeritus of Preaching, Saint Paul School of Theology, Kansas City, Missouri.

Barbara Brown Taylor is Harry R. Butman Professor of Religion and Philosophy, Piedmont College, Demorest, Georgia.

Part 1

A Timeless Question

Harry Emerson Fosdick's
Timeless Question

Mike Graves

I n his introduction to Harry Emerson Fosdick's collection titled *River-side Sermons*, Henry Van Dusen, longtime president of Union Theological Seminary, describes the heyday of Fosdick's ministry at the Riverside Church (1926–46) as "the most influential preaching ministry in the United States in the current century." He writes:

> Sunday by Sunday, throngs crowded into the church, not only from every section of Metropolitan New York but from every corner of the nation and distant parts of the world, overflowing its cathedral-like sanctuary into its chapel and auditorium, filling every room into which the service could be amplified.[1]

Other accounts, including Fosdick's own, testify to the fact that crowds were a part of life at Riverside Church.[2] People often lined up hours early on a Sunday morning, hoping to get in and hear the great orator.

How things have changed! Arriving early to ensure a seat in an overcrowded church, although somewhat common in the late nineteenth and early twentieth centuries, is almost unheard of in the twenty-first century. Of course, it's not that attendance is any barometer for measuring pulpit effectiveness; it never has been. Fosdick himself pointed that out.[3] These days there are simply other options: kids' soccer games, this week's NFL matchup, reading the newspaper, the home show at the convention center, just sleeping in on Sunday morning. The list goes on and on. Things have definitely changed.

In every period it has always been easy to romanticize the so-called "golden age" of preaching, which Clyde Fant contends is always three generations ago. Fant tells how near the end of the nineteenth century, when preachers on both sides of the Atlantic—Charles Haddon Spurgeon, Theodore Parker, Henry Ward Beecher, Alexander Maclaren, and Phillips Brooks—were at "the height of their careers," a spate of articles were published with titles such as "The Decay of Modern Preaching," "Dull Sermons," and "Is the Modern Pulpit a Failure?" Fant concludes that there have always been good preachers, but that the good ones have always been "few and far between."[4] Today, as earlier, despite the good preaching one can find here and there, a question hangs over the church's pulpits: What is the matter with preaching?

That question was the title of an article by Harry Emerson Fosdick: "What Is the Matter with Preaching?" It was published in 1928 in *Harper's Magazine*, of all places, a respected journal known for its timely literary articles. The preacher from New York's famed Riverside Church wrote a piece assessing the then-current status of preaching in America, suggesting among other things that sermons should be relevant to people's needs.[5]

As timely as the article seems when we read it today, it is hard to believe just how long ago Fosdick wrote it. When that July issue of *Harper's* arrived in people's mailboxes, the first all-talking movie, *Lights of New York*, had premiered just three weeks earlier in Manhattan. Calvin Coolidge was in the White House, although Herbert Hoover would be elected in November. That same fall the New York Yankees would win their second World Series in a row, thanks in large part to the batting of Babe Ruth and Lou Gehrig.

As Fosdick called for more relevant sermons, construction on the Empire State Building had yet to begin, and the stock market crash was still a year away. Charles Lindbergh had crossed the Atlantic, but not Amelia Earhart. Ernest Hemingway, F. Scott Fitzgerald, Eugene O'Neill, and Thornton Wilder were the literary buzz, the latter winning that year's Pulitzer Prize in literature for *The Bridge of San Luis Rey*.

More than seventy-five years later, in a much different world, Fosdick's essay is still relevant. He wrote, "This, I take it, is the final test of a sermon's worth: how many individuals wish to see the preacher alone?" In the same essay, he penned the classic line: "Only the preacher proceeds still upon the idea that folk come to church desperately anxious to discover what happened to the Jebusites." What is the matter with preaching? All these years later Fosdick's question is still relevant: What's the matter with preaching *today*?

In reality, good preachers are still few and far between, while questions about the health of preaching are more common than ever. It is hard to find a homiletics book of any sort that does not begin with either a jeremiad or apology on the state of preaching today. Something is indeed wrong in the pulpit. The folks who file into churches wonder why seminaries aren't producing better preachers, and more of them. Some preachers wonder, too. They question why their own preaching isn't better, and what they could do to improve.

This volume hopes to continue the conversation Fosdick initiated all those years ago, including a reprinting of his original essay. Included herein are insights from eleven contemporary scholars. Some of the contributors are, or were, pastors, including Ernest Campbell who was Senior Minister at Riverside from 1968 to 1976. Regrettably, neither William Sloane Coffin, who served Riverside from 1977 to 1987, or James A. Forbes, the church's current Senior Minister, could participate in this project.

Most of the contributors, however, are homileticians (or professors in diverse disciplines) with a keen interest in preaching. Taken together, they address a whole range of topics, from how much easier it is to harp on sin than to announce the gospel's good news (David Bartlett and Mike Graves), to the fact that the very essence of the good news is just that, it is *news*worthy (Tom Long). Some express a degree of prophetic outrage at preachers who are blind to a suffering world, but always faithful to the lectionary (David Buttrick and Ernie Campbell). There is also a prophetic and pastoral reminder that black and white schools of preaching have something to learn from each other (Cleo LaRue).

Some note the mystery of preaching—its poetic qualities so often ignored by pragmatic preachers consumed with a text's meaning (Anna Carter Florence), the way Scripture speaks to the deepest places in listeners (Fred Craddock), or the way in which a sermon's methodology and shape affect the preaching event (Gene Lowry). Others focus on the preachers themselves, who are sometimes what is most wrong with preaching (Marva Dawn) and at other times what is most right, especially when those preachers are in touch with their listeners as well as this pluralistic world in which we live (Barbara Brown Taylor).

All the contributors care deeply about the church's preaching, and all of them tender helpful suggestions for what might be done to improve that preaching. Together, they hope to answer anew Fosdick's timeless question: What is the matter with preaching?

Notes

1. Henry Pitney Van Dusen, "Introduction," in Harry Emerson Fosdick, *Riverside Sermons* (New York: Harper and Brothers, 1958), vii.

2. See, for instance, Fosdick's own recollections in his autobiography, *The Living of These Days* (New York: Harper and Brothers, 1956), 211–12, in which he refers to the temptation to confuse popularity with faithfulness.

3. Ibid.

4. Clyde E. Fant, *Preaching for Today*, rev. ed. (San Francisco: Harper and Row, 1987), 24–27.

5. Two years prior to the publication of his essay, Fosdick expressed similar thoughts in a preface to *Preaching in Theory and Practice*, a homiletics text by Samuel McComb (New York: Oxford, 1926), xii.

What Is the Matter with Preaching?

Harry Emerson Fosdick
(1878–1969)

One might think that such a subject would presuppose preachers as an audience and that an article on it should appear in a magazine devoted to their special interests. On the contrary, there are only about two hundred thousand preachers in the United States, but there are millions who more or less regularly enjoy or endure their ministrations. Whatever, therefore, is the matter with preaching is quantitatively far more a concern of laymen than of clergymen. Moreover if laymen had a clear idea as to the reasons for the futility, dullness, and general ineptitude of so much preaching, they might do something about it. Customers usually have something to say about the quality of goods supplied to them.

Of course, there is no process by which wise and useful discourses can be distilled from unwise and useless personalities, and the ultimate necessity in the ministry, as everywhere else, is sound and intelligent character. "You cannot carve rotten wood," says a Chinese proverb. Every teacher of preaching sometimes feels its truth when he tries to train his students. Whether the grade of intelligence now represented in candidates for the ministry is lower than it used to be cannot easily be determined. As we grow older we tend to idealize the state of things in our youth and to suspect the progressive deterioration of the human race. One theological professor, aged seventy, obviously did this when he told his classes that each new generation of students had known less than their predecessors, and that he was curiously hoping to live to see the next one, which he was certain would know nothing.

This article is reprinted from *Harper's Magazine* (July 1928): 133–41.

The best brains to-day are naturally drawn into occupations other than art, literature, music, education, and religion. These spiritual interests are not the crucial and distinctive concerns of our era. We are magnificent in scientific and commercial exploits but mediocre in affairs of the spirit, and one result is the draining of most of our virile minds into scientific invention and money-making. The ministry of religion suffers along with other kindred callings which serve the souls of men with goodness, truth and beauty. This relative and, I think, temporary inferiority of spiritual callings, however, does not necessarily mean an absolute decline in the intellectual quality of religious leadership; and there is no reason why we should not have much better preaching than we ordinarily get.

One obvious trouble with the mediocre sermon, even when harmless, is that it is uninteresting. It does not matter. It could as well be left unsaid. It produces this effect of emptiness and futility largely because it establishes no connection with the real interests of the congregation. It takes for granted in the minds of the people ways of thinking which are not there, misses the vital concerns which are there, and in consequence uses a method of approach which does not function. It is pathetic to observe the number of preachers who commonly on Sunday speak religious pieces in the pulpit, utterly failing to establish real contact with the thinking or practical interests of their auditors.

Even in the case of a preacher poorly endowed, this state of affairs is unnecessary. No one who has any business to preach at all need preach uninteresting sermons. The fault generally lies, not in the essential quality of the man's mind or character, but in his mistaken methods. He has been wrongly trained or he has blundered into a faulty technic or he never has clearly seen what he should be trying to do in a sermon, and so, having no aim, hits the target only by accident.

No bag of tricks can make a preacher, but if I were to pick out one simple matter of method that would come nearer to making a preacher than any other, it would be the one to which this paper is devoted.

II

Every sermon should have for its main business the solving of some problem—a vital, important problem, puzzling minds, burdening consciences, distracting lives—and any sermon which thus does tackle a real problem, throw even a little light on it, and help some individuals practically to find their way through it cannot be altogether uninteresting.

This endeavor to help people to solve their spiritual problems is a sermon's only justifiable aim. The point of departure and of constant reference, the reason for preaching the sermon in the first place, and the inspiration for its method of approach and the organization of its material should not be something outside the congregation but inside. Within a paragraph or two after a sermon has started, wide areas of any congregation ought to begin recognizing that the preacher is tackling something of vital concern to them. He is handling a subject they are puzzled about, or a way of living they have dangerously experimented with, or an experience that has bewildered them, or a sin that has come perilously near to wrecking them, or an ideal they have been trying to make real, or a need they have not known how to meet. One way or another, they should see that he is engaged in a serious and practical endeavor to state fairly a problem which actually exists in their lives and then to throw what light on it he can.

Any preacher who even with moderate skill is thus helping folk to solve their real problems is functioning. He never will lack an audience. He may have neither eloquence nor learning, but he is doing the one thing that is a preacher's business. He is delivering the goods that the community has a right to expect from the pulpit as much as it has a right to expect shoes from a cobbler. And if any preacher is not doing this, even though he have at his disposal both erudition and oratory, he is not functioning at all.

Many preachers, for example, indulge habitually in what they call expository sermons. They take a passage from Scripture and, proceeding on the assumption that the people attending church that morning are deeply concerned about what the passage means, they spend their half hour or more on historical exposition of the verse or chapter, ending with some appended practical application to the auditors. Could any procedure be more surely predestined to dullness and futility? Who seriously supposes that, as a matter of fact, one in a hundred of the congregation cares, to start with, what Moses, Isaiah, Paul, or John meant in those special verses, or came to church deeply concerned about it? Nobody else who talks to the public so assumes that the vital interests of the people are located in the meaning of words spoken two thousand years ago. The advertisers of any goods, from a five-foot shelf of classic books to the latest life insurance policy, plunge as directly as possible after contemporary wants, felt needs, actual interests and concerns. Even moving picture producers, if they present an ancient tale, like Tristan and Isolde, are likely to begin with a modern girl reading the story. Somehow or other, every other agency dealing with the public recognizes that contact with the actual life of the auditor is the one place to begin. Only the preacher proceeds still upon the idea that folk come to church desperately anxious to discover what happened to the Jebusites. The result is that folk less and less come to church at all.

This does not mean that the Bible has either lost or lessened its value to the preacher. It means that preachers who pick out texts from the Bible and then proceed to give their historic settings, their logical meaning in the context, their place in the theology of the writer, with a few practical reflections appended, are grossly misusing the Bible. The Scripture is an amazing compendium of experiments in human life under all sorts of conditions, from the desert to cosmopolitan Rome, and with all sorts of theories, from the skepticism of Ecclesiastes to the faith of John. It is incalculably rich in insight and illumination. It has light to shed on all sorts of human problems now and always; and, as for the personality of Jesus, if Rodin, the modern sculptor, could feel that Phidias, the Greek sculptor, could never be equaled—"No artist will ever surpass Phidias—for progress exists in the world, but not in art. The greatest of sculptors . . . will remain forever without an equal"—it is surely open to even the most radical of Christians to adore Christ as Master and Lord.

What all the great writers of Scripture, however, were interested in was human living, and the modern preacher who honors them should start with that, should clearly visualize some real need, perplexity, sin, or desire in his auditors, and then should throw on the problem all the light he can find in the Scripture or anywhere else. No matter what one's theory about the Bible is, this is the effective approach to preaching. The Bible is a searchlight, not so much intended to be looked at as to be thrown upon a shadowed spot.

That much insight into contemporary human problems which almost all preachers use in thinking about the practical applications at the end of their sermons might do some good if it were used, instead, at the beginning of their sermons. Let them not end but start with thinking of the auditors' vital needs, and then let the whole sermon be organized around their constructive endeavor to meet those needs.

III

An increasing number of preachers, too modern by far to use the old, authoritative, textual method which we have just described, do not on that account light on a better one. They turn to what is called topical preaching. They search contemporary life in general and the newspapers in particular for subjects. They discover that in comparison with dry, textual analysis there is such attractive vividness in handling present-day themes, such as divorce, Bolshevism, America's Nicaraguan policy, the new aviation, or the latest book, that they enjoy their own preaching better, and more people come to hear it. It is at least a matter of contemporary and not archeological interest.

The nemesis of such a method, however, is not far off. Most preachers who try it fall ultimately into their own trap. Watch the records of any considerable number of them and see how large a proportion peter out and leave the ministry altogether. Instead of starting with a text, they start with their own ideas on some subject of their choice, but their ideas on that subject may be much farther away from the vital interests of the people than a great text from the Bible. Indeed, the fact that history has thought it worth while to preserve the text for so many centuries would cause a gambling man to venture largely on the text's superior vitality.

Week after week one sees these topical preachers who turn their pulpits into platforms and their sermons into lectures, straining after some new, intriguing subject; and one knows that in private they are straining after some new, intriguing ideas about it. One knows also that no living man can weekly produce first-hand, independent, and valuable judgments on such an array of diverse themes, covering the whole range of human life. And, deeper yet, one who listens to such preaching or reads it knows that the preacher is starting at the wrong end. He is thinking first of his ideas, original or acquired, when he should think first of his people. He is organizing his sermon around the elucidation of his theme, whereas he should organize it around the endeavor to meet his people's need. He is starting with a subject whereas he should start with an object. His one business is with the real problems of these individual people in his congregation. Nothing that he says on any subject, however wise and important, matters much unless it makes at the beginning vital contact with the practical life and daily thinking of the audience.

This idea that we are applying to preaching is simply the project method, which is recognized as the basis of all good modern teaching. The old pedagogy saw on one side the child, as a passive receptacle, and on the other side a subject, like mathematics or geography, waiting to be learned, and, so seeing the situation, proceeded to pour the subject, willy-nilly, into the child. If he resisted, he was punished; if he failed to assimilate it, he was accounted stupid. No good teacher today could tolerate such an idea or method. The question now is why the child should wish to know geography and what practical interest in the child's life can be appealed to in the endeavor to have him desire to know geography. Modern pedagogy starts, not with the subject, but with the child. It adapts what is to be learned to the learner rather than vice versa. Even the food which the child eats for breakfast, coming from the ends of the earth, is used to fascinate his interest in other lands; and we find our children getting at their mathematics by measuring the cubic space of the front parlor, or estimating the distance per second which they have walked in an hour.

All this is good sense and good psychology. Everybody else is using it from first-class teachers to first-class advertisers. Why should so many preachers continue in such belated fashion to neglect it? The people often blindly know that there is something the matter with the sermon although they cannot define it. The text was good and the truth was undeniable. The subject was well chosen and well developed but, for all that, nothing happened. The effect was flat. So far as the sermon was concerned, the congregation might as well have stayed home. It may have been a "beautiful effort," as some kindly woman doubtless told the preacher, but it did no business in human lives. The reason for this can commonly be traced to one cause: the preacher started his sermon at the wrong end. He made it the exposition of a text or the elucidation of a subject instead of a well-planned endeavor to help solve some concrete problems in the individual lives before him. He need not have used any other text or any different materials in his sermon, but if he had defined his object rightly he would have arranged and massed the material differently. He would have gone into his sermon via real interest in his congregation and would have found the whole procedure kindling to himself and to them.

IV

The meaning of this method can best be seen in some of its corollaries. For one thing, it makes a sermon a co-operative enterprise between the preacher and his congregation. When a man has got hold of a real difficulty in the life and thinking of his people and is trying to meet it he finds himself not so much dogmatically thinking for them as co-operatively thinking with them. His sermon is an endeavor to put himself in their places and help them to think their way through.

The difference in tone and quality which this makes in a sermon is incalculable. Anyone accustomed to hearing preaching must be aware of two diverse effects commonly produced. One type of minister plays "Sir Oracle." He is dogmatic, assertive, uncompromising. He flings out his dicta as though to say to all hearers, Take it or leave it. He has settled the matter concerning which he is speaking and is not asking our opinion; he is telling us. This homiletical dogmatism has its own kind of influence on credulous and impressionable minds. Such minds are numerous, so that such preaching can go on for years ahead. As Jesus said about the Pharisees, such preachers have their reward.

Their method, however, has long since lost its influence over intelligent people, and the future does not belong to it. The future, I think, belongs to a type of sermon which can best be described as an adventure in co-operative thinking between the preacher and his congregation. The impression made by such preaching easily is felt by anyone who runs into it. The preacher takes hold of a real problem in our lives and, stating it better than we could state it, goes on to deal with it fairly, frankly, helpfully. The result is inevitable: he makes us think. We may agree with him or disagree with him, but we must follow him. He is dealing with something vital to us and so he makes us think with him even though we may have planned a far more somnolent use of sermon time.

Here, too, we are dealing with preaching in terms of good pedagogy. The lecture method of instruction is no longer in the ascendent. To be sure, there are subjects which must be handled by the positive setting forth of information in a lecture, but more and more, good teaching is discussional, co-operative. The instructor does not so much think for the students as think with them. From the desire to use some such method in religious instruction has come the forum in modern churches and the questionnaire group after the sermon, where those who wish can put objections and inquiries to the preacher, and discussion groups of all sorts where religious questions are threshed out in mutual conference. The principle behind such methods is psychologically right. We never really get an idea until we have thought it for ourselves.

A good sermon should take this into account. A wise preacher can so build his sermon that it will be, not a dogmatic monologue but a co-operative dialogue in which all sorts of things in the minds of the congregation—objections, questions, doubts, and confirmations—will be brought to the front and fairly dealt with. This requires clairvoyance on the preacher's part as to what the people are thinking, but any man who lacks that has no business to preach anyway.

Recently, in a school chapel, so I am told, the headmaster was only well started on his sermon when a professor mounted the pulpit beside him and offered a criticism of what he was saying. Great excitement reigned. The headmaster answered the objection, but the professor remained in the pulpit, and the sermon that day was a running discussion between the two on a great theme in religion. To say that the boys were interested is to put it mildly. They never had been so worked up over anything religious before. It turned out afterward that the whole affair had been pre-arranged. It was an experiment in a new kind of preaching, where one man does not produce a monologue but where diverse and competing points of view are frankly dealt with.

Any preacher without introducing another personality outwardly in the pulpit can utilize the principle involved in this method. If he is to handle helpfully real problems in his congregation, he must utilize it. He must see clearly and state fairly what people other than himself are thinking on the matter in hand. He may often make this so explicit as to begin paragraphs with such phrases as, "But some of you will say," or "Let us consider a few questions that inevitably arise," or, "Face frankly with me the opposing view," or, "Some of you have had experiences that seem to contradict what we are saying." Of course, this method, like any other, can be exaggerated and become a mannerism. But something like it is naturally involved in any preaching which tries to help people to think through and live through their problems.

Such preaching when it is well done always possesses an important quality. It is not militant and pugnacious but irenic, kindly, and constructively helpful. How much the churches need such discourses! We have endless sermons of sheer propaganda where preachers set out by hook or crook to put something over on the congregation. We have pugnacious sermons where preachers wage campaigns, attack enemies, assail the citadels of those who disagree and in general do anything warlike and vehement. But sermons that try to face the people's real problems with them, meet their difficulties, answer their questions, interpret their experiences in sympathetic, wise, and understanding co-operation—what a dearth of them there is!

Yet not only is such preaching the most useful; it is the most interesting. This is the only way I know to achieve excitement without sensationalism. Constructively to state the problem of meeting trouble victoriously, or of living above the mediocre moral level of a modern city, or of believing in God in the face of the world's evil, or of making Christ's principles triumphant against the present international and interracial prejudice is surely not sensationalism, but it is vitally interesting. A breathless auditor came up after one such sermon saying, "I nearly passed out with excitement, for I did not see how you possibly could answer that objection which you raised against your own thought. I supposed you would do it somehow but I could not see how until you did it." There is nothing that people are so interested in as themselves, their own problems, and the way to solve them. That fact is basic. No preaching that neglects it can raise a ripple on a congregation. It is the primary starting point of all successful public speaking, and for once the requirements of practical success and ideal helpfulness coincide. He who really helps folk to understand their own lives and see their way through their spiritual problems is performing one of the most important functions in the modern world.

V

No method of preaching is without its dangers and, of course, this one which I am espousing has perils in plenty. I presented it once to a group of experienced ministers and collected a galaxy of warnings as to its possible perversions. They thought of times when they had tried it with disappointing results. They had endeavored so precisely to deal with a real problem that Mr. Smith had vexatiously waked up to the fact that they were talking about him, or they had wanted to be so fair about objections to their thought that they had overstated the opposing side and then had neither time nor ability to answer it, or they had been so practical in thinking about some definite problem that they had become trivial and had forgotten to bring the wide sweep of the Gospel's truth to bear in an elevating way on the point at issue, or they had been so anxious to deal with felt needs in the congregation that they forgot to arouse the consciousness of need unfelt but real. All these dangers are present in the method which we are suggesting. It can be offensively personal, argumentatively unconvincing, practically trivial, and narrowed to the conscious needs of mediocre people. But these perversions are the fault of just such unskilled handling as would wreck any method whatsoever.

The best antidote to making a wrong use of the project method in the pulpit is to be discovered in the ideal of creative preaching. The danger involved in starting a sermon with a problem is that the very word problem suggests something to be merely debated and its solution may suggest nothing more than the presentation of a helpful idea to the mind. But we all want something else in a sermon than a discussion even about one of our vital problems, no matter how wise the discussion or how suggestive the conclusion. The best sermons, I still maintain, are preached on the project method but, after all, in the preacher's hands it means something more than the same method in a classroom. It is the project method plus.

What this plus is can easily be seen. When a preacher deals with joy, let us say, he ought to start, not with joy in the fifth century B.C. nor with joy as a subject to be lectured on, but with the concrete difficulties in living joyfully that his people actually experience. He should have in mind from the start their mistaken ideas of joy, their false attempts to get it, the causes of their joylessness, and their general problem of victorious and happy living in the face of life's puzzling and sometimes terrific experiences. This is a real problem for everybody, and the sermon that throws light on it is a real sermon. But that real sermon must do more than discuss joy—it must produce it. All powerful preaching is creative. It actually brings to pass in the lives of the congregation the thing it talks about. So to tackle the problem of joy that the whole congregation goes out more joyful than it came in—that is the mark of a genuine sermon.

Here lies a basic distinction between a sermon and an essay. The outstanding criticism popularly and properly launched against a great deal of our modern, liberal preaching is that though it consists of neat, analytical discourses, pertinent to real problems and often well conceived and well phrased, it does nothing to anybody. Such sermons are not sermons but essays. It is lamentably easy to preach feebly about repentance without making anybody feel like repenting, or to deliver an accomplished discourse on peace without producing any of that valuable article in the auditors. On the other hand, a true preacher is creative. He does more than discuss a subject; he produces the thing itself in the people who hear it. As an English bishop said about Phillips Brooks, "He makes one feel so strong."

Obviously, personal quality is the major factor in producing spiritual power. There is a real reason for the halos which the painters have put about the heads of the saints. They are symbols of something intangible but real—an effluence that ordinary men do not possess, a radiance that is not the less powerful because it is ineffable.

Nevertheless, even a moderately endowed preacher, who never would suggest a halo to anybody, may have some of this power to create what he discusses. Whether he does or not depends a great deal upon whether he sees the objective clearly enough to head for it with precision. If he thinks of his sermon merely as a discussion of somebody's problem he will play with a series of ideas, but if he thinks of his sermon as an endeavor to create something in his congregation he will play on motives. There is where much of our modern preaching fails. The old preachers at their best did know where the major motives were. Fear, love, gratitude, self-preservation, altruism—such springs of human action the old sermons often used with consummate power. To be sure, they sometimes outraged the personalities of both adults and children by the way they did it but, for all that, they often showed an uncanny insight into the springs of human action. I often think that we modern preachers talk about psychology a great deal more than our predecessors did but use it a great deal less.

One often reads modern sermons with amazement. How do the preachers expect to get anything done in human life with such discourses? They do not come within reaching distance of any powerful motives in man's conduct. They are keyed to argumentation rather than creation. They produce essays, which means that they are chiefly concerned with the elucidation of a theme. If they were producing sermons they would be chiefly concerned with the transformation of personality.

This, however, brings us back to our major issue. If a preacher is to use the project method, as a preacher should, not simply to discuss the real problems of real people but to create in the people the thing that is discussed, his chief interest must be the individuals in his congregation. He must know them through and through, not only their problems but their motives, not only what they are thinking but why they are acting as they do. Preaching becomes thrilling business when it successfully achieves this definite direction and aim. A sermon, then, is an engineering operation by which a chasm is spanned so that spiritual goods on one side are actually transported into personal lives upon the other. *The bridge*

VI

Throughout this paper we have held up the ideal of preaching as an interesting operation. That is a most important matter, not only to the audience but to the man in the pulpit. The number of fed-up, fatigued, bored preachers is appalling. Preaching has become to them a chore. They have to "get up" a sermon, perhaps two sermons, weekly. They struggle at it. The juice goes out of them as the years pass. They return repeatedly to old subjects and try to whip up enthusiasm over weather-beaten texts and themes. Their discourses sink into formality. They build conventional sermon outlines, fill them in with conventional thoughts, and let it go at that. Where is the zest and thrill with which in their chivalrous youth they started out to be ministers of Christ to the spiritual life of their generation?

Of course, nothing can make preaching easy. At best it means drenching a congregation with one's lifeblood. But while, like all high work, it involves severe concentration, toil, and self-expenditure, it can be so exhilarating as to recreate in the preacher the strength it takes from him, as good agriculture replaces the soil it uses. Whenever that phenomenon happens one is sure to find a man predominantly interested in personalities and what goes on inside of them. He has understood people, their problems, troubles, motives, failures, and desires, and in his sermons he has known how to handle their lives so vitally that week after week he has produced real changes. People have habitually come up after the sermon, not to offer some bland compliment, but to say, "How did you know I was facing that problem only this week?" or "We were discussing that very matter at dinner last night," or, best of all, "I think you would understand my case—may I have a personal interview with you?"

This, I take it, is the final test of a sermon's worth: how many individuals wish to see the preacher alone?

I should despair, therefore, of any man's sustained enthusiasm and efficiency in the pulpit if he were not in constant, confidential relationship with individuals. Personal work and preaching are twins. As I watch some preachers swept off their feet by the demands of their own various organizations, falling under the spell of bigness, and rushing from one committee to another to put over some new scheme to enlarge the work or save the world, I do not wonder at the futility which so often besets them. They are doing everything except their chief business, for that lies inside individuals.

If someone utterly "sold" to our American worship of size and our grandiose schemes for saving the world should protest that this means individualistic preaching, he would only reveal his own obtuseness. In one sense, all good preaching and all good public speaking of any kind must be individualistic—it must establish vital contact with individuals. Even if one were speaking on the rings of Saturn one might as well not begin unless one could cook up some reason why the audience should wish to hear about them. The failure to recognize this fact explains why so much of our so-called social preaching falls flat or rouses resentment. A man who on Sunday morning starts in to solve the economic question or the international question as though his people must have come that day of a purpose to hear him do it deserves almost any unpleasant thing that can happen to him. He may be a Ph.D. in psychology but I doubt whether he knows enough about the way men's minds do actually act to be a successful grocer's assistant.

His special business as a Christian preacher with economic and international questions is profound and vital, but in so far as he sticks to his last his interest as a minister is distinct from anyone else's and it calls for an approach of his own. The world's economic and international situation is not alien to our personal problems. It invades them, shapes them in multitudinous ways; it undoes in us and around us much that the Christian should wish done and it does much that the Christian most should fight against. Let a preacher, therefore, start at the end of the problem where he belongs. Let him begin with the people in front of him, with what goes on inside of them because social conditions are as they are, with the economic and international reasons for many of their unchristian moods, tempers, ideas, and ideals, with their responsibilities and obligations in the matter, and in general with the tremendous stake which personal Christianity has in those powerful social forces which create the climate in which it must either live or die. Such preaching on social questions starts, as it should start, with the individuals immediately concerned, establishes contact with their lives, and has at least some faint chance of doing a real business on Sunday.

Every problem that the preacher faces thus leads back to one basic question: how well does he understand the thoughts and lives of his people? That he should know his Gospel goes without saying, but he may know it ever so well and yet fail to get it within reaching distance of anybody unless he intimately understands people and cares more than he cares for anything else what is happening inside of them. Preaching is wrestling with individuals over questions of life and death, and until that idea of it commands a preacher's mind and method, eloquence will avail him little and theology not at all.

Part 2

What's the Matter with Preaching Today?

Chapter One

Showing Mercy

David L. Bartlett

In a recent study of the works of the novelist P. D. James, Ralph C. Wood describes a problem that James faces as a novelist:

> James confesses, regretfully, that evil is much easier to depict than good. A stolen cache, a slashed throat, a slandered reputation—these all attract immediate interest. Goodness, by contrast is enormously difficult to give vibrant fictional life. Precisely because it is often quiet and undramatic, James explains, charity is hard to make artistically compelling. There is not much artistic possibility to be found in caring for a sick friend, enduring an unhappy marriage, performing uncongenial work. Such deeds present an acute theological problem as well. . . . Our loss of belief in the transcendent Witness and Vindicator has come at an awful cost.[1]

Old Testament scholar (and preacher) Sibley Towner once remarked that too much preaching presents sin and evil in vivid, narrative, Anglo-Saxon English and then presents grace in Latin abstractions. Towner's more exact description was that when we preach, we often present sin with the vividness of 1 and 2 Samuel and grace with the abstractions of St. Paul. I shall suggest below that Paul can help with vividness too, but I affirm the widespread problem if not Towner's exact description.

Similarly, it is now a commonplace of English literary studies that Satan is far more interesting than God in *Paradise Lost*, and probably more interesting than Adam and Eve as well. In part this is because Milton can move to vivid, concrete imagery for Satan without the kind of reverential distance reserved for God. In part it's because Satan is active while God is contemplative, a kind of divine tenured professor. In part, I suppose, it's because most of us readers identify instantly with Satan's pride rather than with God's providential benevolence. Consider, for example, when Satan who has been cast down speaks unforgettable poetry:

> Farewell happy Fields,
> Where Joy for ever dwells: Hail horrors, hail
> Infernal world, and thou profoundest Hell
> Receive thy new Possessor: One who brings
> A mind not to be chang'd by Place or Time.
> The mind is its own place, and in itself
> Can make a Heav'n of Hell, a Hell of Heav'n.
> What matter where, if I be still the same,
> And what I should be, all but less than he
> Whom Thunder hath made greater? Here at least
> We shall be free; th'Almighty hath not built
> Here for his envy, will not drive us hence:
> Here we may reign secure, and in my choice
> To reign is worth ambition though in Hell:
> Better to reign in Hell, than serve in Heav'n.[2]

Later in *Paradise Lost*, God the Father and God the Son have a dialogue in which they meditate on how best to reverse Satan's evil and human sin. Theologically the plan is flawless; dramatically it doesn't quite rise to Satan's embodied rhetoric:

> So Man, as is most just,
> Shall satisfy for Man, be judg'd and die,
> And dying rise, and rising with him raise
> His Brethren, ransomed with his own dear life.
> So Heavn'ly love shall outdo Hellish hate.[3]

Or recall Jonathan Edwards's most acclaimed sermon, "Sinners in the Hands of an Angry God," which we remember in part because that image of the poor sinner dangling like a spider on the thinnest of webs over the threat of eternal damnation is vivid:

> O sinner! Consider the fearful danger you are in: 'tis a great furnace
> of wrath, a wide and bottomless pit, full of the fire of wrath, that you
> are held over in the hand of that God, whose wrath is provoked and

incensed as much against you as against many of the damned in hell: you hang by a slender thread, with the flames of divine wrath flashing about it, and ready every moment to singe it, and burn it asunder; and you have no interest in any mediator, and nothing to lay hold of to save yourself, nothing to keep off the flames of wrath, nothing of your own, nothing that you have ever done, nothing that you can do, to induce God to spare you one moment.[4]

Edwards also wrote wonderful sermons on the beauty of God and the delight of faith, but those have faded from our collective consciousness. Look at this paragraph from the sermon entitled "The Pleasantness of Religion" and get a different sense of Edwards and of the possibilities of preaching:

Ps. 84:10, "A day in thy courts is better than a thousand elsewhere." The Christian spends every day as it were in the courts of God. The very pledge that God has given to the godly as an earnest of the reward, is such that it's well worth the while to deny all the pleasures of sin and to take all the troubles of religion for it. Rev. 2:17, "To him that overcometh will I give to eat of the hidden manna, and will give him a white stone, and in the stone a new name written, which no man knoweth save he that receiveth it." What pure delight have the godly in [this life]. How great, then, is the reward of the righteous, if they have such a great reward in the life to come, and so great a reward in this life in the bargain.[5]

What's the matter with preaching today? It would seem that sin appears more interesting than grace, evil more lively than goodness. The dilemma is not new, but it's nonetheless a dilemma. So what shall we do about it? The old admonition of our creative writing teachers holds for preaching as much as for short stories: show; don't tell. But for the most part we *show* evil and then *tell about* goodness. We *show* judgment and then *talk about* the doctrine of mercy. I do not think this is an insoluble dilemma, and so I want to make some suggestions about models for showing mercy, not just talking about it.

The Catalog of Evil and the Announcement of Grace

The devotion to showing sin and then telling about mercy takes a particular form in the sermons of many novice preachers. The sermon begins with the catalog of evil. The preacher sounds like that catalog of distress in Mark 13, but without any attention to the apocalyptic promise. The preacher announces, "Internationally there are wars and rumors of war; in our nation there is growing poverty; divorce rates are climbing; crime abounds. Nor have we found a cure for cancer." I have heard eight minutes of a fifteen-minute sermon go down the laundry list of contemporary woes. One of two things happens to the congregation. Either they become so overwhelmed by the list of evils that there is no way for the last seven minutes to begin to bail them out, or they simply tune out because they, too, have read the newspaper and watched the evening news. The preacher presents herself with an impossible task, there is no way that any single doctrine, affirmation, story, or poem can reverse the multiplicity of distress.

There is much we can learn from the effectiveness of Harry Emerson Fosdick's preaching, and one thing we can learn is that he took on the world one evil at a time. When he dealt with psychological fear, he dealt with fear, not with fear, infidelity, and psychological depression.

> We may be sure that every one here, one way or another, faces the problem of fear. If someone says that he does not, a skilled confessor of souls, I think, would take his word for that only temporarily, pending further investigation. Fear runs so far back into the human heritage, takes such diverse forms, works its way out to such disguised results, that nobody, however normal, altogether escapes it. As for the abnormal, one of the leading psychiatrists of the world has said: "If fear were abolished from modern life, the work of the psychotherapist would be nearly gone."[6]

When Fosdick dealt with war and peace (as World War II approached) he dealt with that, not with war, peace, the decline in sexual mores, and the dangers of addictive gambling. And he dealt with the issue at some length, in some detail and specificity:

> The dictatorships say, War! so we say, War! They build vast armaments, so we build vast armaments. Step by step, day by day, we become their yes-men. They say, Dictatorial control of the nation for the sake of war's efficiency! So in Washington we propose bills that provide on the day of war's declaration, that the nation shall conscript life, property, labor conscience.[7]

Because he dealt with hugely important problems, but dealt with them one at a time, the specific weight of the "solution" was roughly analogous to the weight of the issue. There may not be any way to respond to all the world's ills in one morning, but there are things that a wise pastor can say about fear and anxiety that will make a difference. And there are words that a faithful preacher can bring about war that bear witness, that make us think anew and maybe act anew as well.

Fosdick's words on war, for instance, may not fit our theology, but they are homiletically clear, direct, and memorable:

> Then there is undeserved goodness, where we have been unworthy, generous, unkind, unjust, and lo! some one comes back at us with good-will and friendliness.
>
> From the days at home when our parents so treated us, through all our lives, no force has reached so deep, laid hold so hard, lifted so powerfully as that. Thank God not everybody has slapped back at us! Thank God some people did go the second mile with us! The salvation of the world depends on the multiplication of people who understand and practice that adventurous ethic.[8]

One way to tackle the dilemma of preaching as bad news is to limit the badness we try to deal with on any particular day. Sufficient unto the day is the evil thereof, said our Lord, and sufficient to most Sundays is careful, thoughtful attention to one issue that tests the faithfulness of our people.

Picturing Transcendence

As Ralph Wood's review of P. D. James's work suggests, one of our problems is that we are practically, if not theologically, committed to "realism." And "realistically" there is no problem in describing distress or loss or evil. The problem is that artistic and philosophical realism, by definition, leave out the transcendent. Realism arose as a literary movement precisely to show what could be captured by a strictly empirical, day to day, unflinching description of life in all its frequent disappointments and even squalor.[9]

The Bible, of course, is the oddest combination of "realism" and "transcendence." The realistic sins of Cain are judged and in part redeemed by a word from an invisible God, and the realistic sins of David are judged and in part redeemed by a word from an all too audible prophet. Blindness, epilepsy, something very like paranoid schizophrenia are described by Mark's Gospel with realism that would suit Émile Zola. But what has realism to do with prayer, supplication, promise, and healing, all of which are every bit as prominent in Mark as dramatic disaster?

I sometimes think that the movies have done a better job of capturing transcendence than sermons have. There is that astonishing moment in *Places in the Heart* where the table at the Lord's Supper opens up across time and space and welcomes the communion of saints. The film *Magnolia* tells us from the start that it is a story of the way in which different lives are drawn together in a web of meaning that transcends each individual story. Janet Maslin, a reviewer not unsympathetic to religious perspectives, nonetheless finds that this movie goes too far:

> The great uh-oh moment in Paul Thomas Anderson's *Magnolia* occurs about two-thirds of the way through this artfully orchestrated symphony of L.A. stories. A song bursts out: it is heard first from one character, then from another, until all the film's assorted lost souls are brought together by a single anxiety-ridden refrain.[10]

Of course having all those separate characters in their separate places singing the same song is not exactly "realistic," but neither is the interweaving of a dozen different stories into one symphonylike whole symphony "realistic." Neither are Hamlet's soliloquies, the way Shakespeare hints at the transcendent issues behind his revenge story, "realistic." And heaven knows real-life gangs in New York did not, even in the '50s, join in contrapuntal song and dance as they do in *West Side Story*. But if it is "real" that God is God, then artists and preachers alike have the right and obligation to find the pictures by which we note the extraordinary that shapes and illuminates the ordinary. And we don't do that just by talking about the doctrine of incarnation, but by incarnating.

I am far too modern to understand postmodernism, but I do think I get one thing. "Realism" is not necessarily the only way to describe what's real. It is a philosophical position posing as a universal principle. I doubt if our preaching or our congregations (or perhaps even our theology) is ready for many premodern references to angels, and in the congregations where I preach, at least, it is sometimes hard even to make a case for miracles. But I do not think it is nuts to believe that on occasion, explicitly or implicitly, very different people driven by a providence they do not see, sing the same song, play parts in the same drama. Preaching needs sometimes to push the envelope.

Deliver Us from Bathos

On the other hand, the dogmas of realism may help us to avoid a besetting sin of the sermonic story, namely, sentimentality. Alas, it is not enough for a story to be true unless it is also truthful. There is one of those generic sermon illustrations that I have heard twice and therefore twice too often. I could not find it in my Web search, which is a good sign. The story is intended to help us understand the atonement, and it goes something like this.

A father is in charge of a railroad bridge over a rapid and dangerous river. His job is to work the devices that close the bridge when a train is approaching but to open the bridge, presumably for boat traffic, when no train is in sight. Here's the sad scene: Father hears a train approaching and gets ready to throw the switch, when he notices that his son is playing on the coupling of the bridge. Papa knows that if he fails to throw the switch the train, a passenger train filled with innocent people, will plunge into the river. But if he throws the switch, his son will be tossed from the bridge to certain death. Papa pulls the switch. Atonement.

What's wrong with this story? Plenty! Theologically it makes the father unspeakably absentminded (how did the son wander off like that?). Soteriologically it makes the son entirely passive: the accidental savior. But humanly and artistically the story is also off base. This is not the transcendent emerging in the midst of the ordinary, but the perversely unlikely posing as redemptive.

I know no absolute remedy for sentimental stories, but I have a few prophylactic helps. Avoid the generic illustration: "The story is told. . . ." If you don't know who told it or about whom it was told, it runs the danger of sentimentality. Avoid illustrative "helps," whether from books or from the Internet. The reality of a story or image depends in part on its being genuinely anchored. That means the quotation from a book should be anchored in the larger context of the book, the pithy biographical anecdote in the larger context of the subject's life, the thought anchored in the preacher's intellectual life, not somebody else's thought conveniently pithy and harvested for this occasion alone. It is easy enough to anchor our diagnosis in plausible reality; our comforts will be comfortable to the extent that they are anchored in real life, real thought, extensive reading.

Back to the Bible

Erich Auerbach has written of the particular combination of reticence and mystery that marks the most memorable biblical passages. Brevity and directness build literary and homiletical power too. This is true as well for grace as for judgment.

> From the very first, in the Old Testament stories, the sublime, tragic, and problematic take shape precisely in the domestic and common-place: scenes such as those between Cain and Abel, between Noah and his sons, between Abraham, Sarah, and Hagar, between Rebekah, Jacob, and Esau, and so on, are inconceivable in the Homeric style. The entirely different ways of developing conflicts are enough to account for this. In the Old Testament stories the peace of daily life in the house, in the fields, and among the flocks, is undermined by jeal-ousy over election and the promise of a blessing, and complications arise which would have been utterly incomprehensible to the Homer-ic heroes. . . . The sublime influence of God here reaches so deeply into the everyday that the two realms of the sublime and the everyday are not only actually unseparated but basically inseparable.[11]

Furthermore, suggests Auerbach, in the great biblical stories both the divine initiative and the human response are presented with a kind of aes-thetic reticence:

> The personages speak in the Bible story, too; but their speech does not serve, as does speech in Homer, to manifest, to externalize thoughts—on the contrary, it serves to indicate thoughts which remain unexpressed; Abraham, receiving the command, says nothing and does what he has been told to do. The conversation between Abraham and Isaac on the way to the place of sacrifice is only an inter-ruption of the heavy silence and makes it all the more burden-some. . . . Everything remains unexpressed.[12]

Even Paul, who is accused of abstractness, can be at once perfectly and modestly concrete. "Therefore, to keep me from being too elated, a thorn was given me in the flesh, a messenger of Satan to torment me, to keep me from being too elated. Three times I appealed to the Lord about this, that it would leave me" (2 Cor. 12:7–8). Our temptation would be to describe the genesis, diagnosis, and prognosis for the thorn, list the variety of spe-cialists we consulted and reproduce for the congregation a full transcript of our petitionary prayers. Paul is the model of the preacher who uses him-self as witness to the grace which he preaches, but does so with sufficient reticence that we always remember, or almost always remember, that what he preaches is the grace and not himself. The understandable reluctance ever to bring self into sermon is a reaction, I think, to preaching as therapy for the preacher, on the one hand, or as autohagiography on the other. Paul gives us a different model of the way in which he bears witness to the truth by which he has been saved: Look at me glancingly so that you may look at Christ gladly.

The Gospels, of course, provide inestimable instances of mercy narrated, shown, not told. In the Gospels the gospel does become a story, with the transcendence and the ordinary mixed together somewhat differently in each Gospel. In the mininarratives, like the prodigal son story, we know enough but not too much. What precipitated the rush toward the far country? How had older and younger brother gotten along in their childhood years? Did the younger son really consort with prostitutes or did the older make that one up? Long journey away; painful journey home, either from the far country or from the nearby field. Longing father. Enough.

In the longer story of the Gospels, notice what we are not told. We are spared those sermons that describe the exact nature of crucifixion down to each grisly medical detail. Even resurrection is told with no trumpets and minimal trappings, and however many or few the accouterments of nativity, at the story's heart is still a newborn human child.

Mercy is imaged, too. It is not only narrative, but poetry, that carries the power. "The Lord is my shepherd." "Consider the lilies of the field." "I am the bread of life." On the whole the most powerful biblical images are neither as complicated as John Donne nor as flatfooted as Edgar A. Guest. My own somewhat considered bias is that the most Bible-like poet is not an especially religious one, but Robert Frost, because his simply described tangible world sometimes touches on a world less tangible but no less real: "Come with rain, O loud Southwester!/Bring the singer, bring the nester. . . ." Or his better-known line from another piece, "The woods are lovely, dark and deep,/But I have promises to keep. . . ."[13] The best biblical imagery is also lovely, dark, deep, and appropriately repetitive.

All this is to say that I do not think the Bible has what Ralph Wood described as P. D. James's problem or Milton's either. The biblical Satan is not nearly as interesting, multifaceted, clever, or funny as the biblical God, the protagonist of the long story.[14] Peter is a lot more interesting than Judas, and not just because he gets better lines. David and Absalom are both complicated, but one drives complication toward mercy and the other toward damnation, and I don't think the more hopeful story is the duller one. In addition to all the things we want to say about Jesus from the side of faith, from the side of sheer press worthiness, there is no end to the books that have been written, or will be written, about him. So why should our preaching turn him into the subject of propositions instead of the protagonist of stories, the lover of our souls?[15]

Getting Specific

The biblical precedents for showing mercy and not just talking about it have parallels in our contemporary lives and literature. Paul's willingness to use himself as witness for the gospel is reimagined by Frederick Buechner, whose most powerful books and sermons are bold to take his own story as a model of the way in which grace intersects biography. He writes, "I have found more and more that, like the back pages, it is in the interior where the real news is." He adds:

> I have come to believe that by and large the human family all has the same secrets, which are both very telling and very important to tell. . . . It is important to tell our secrets too because it makes it easier that way to see where we have been and where we are going. It also makes it easier for other people to tell us a secret or two of their own, and exchanges like that have a lot to do with what being a family is all about and what being human is all about. Finally, I suspect that it is by entering that deep place inside us where our secrets are kept that we come perhaps closer than we do anywhere else to the One who, whether we realize it or not, is of all our secrets the most telling and the most precious we have to tell.[16]

Borrowing from Buechner's example (though not trying to imitate his prose) we have not only the right but the obligation to attend to our stories to see where God has been present. Had God not been present we would not be in this business, the preaching business, of course, but most importantly the Christian business. We know that, but sometimes it will help our congregations if we say so.

We can balance the danger of total theological self-absorption by attending to other people's stories. Sometimes, of course, we will want to attend to the heroes of the faith, partly because they make God's activity visible, partly because they are members with us of the communion of saints and attention should be paid. I do preach Augustine and Luther and Francis and St. Theresa and Mother Teresa, too. But there is always the danger that we will signal that faith is only for the astonishing or, God help us, only for the ordained. So we listen to other lives, especially to the lives of the people in our own church. We never violate confidence, and we never tell a story without checking with the one who told us, but concrete stories with concrete names do help overcome Ralph Wood's aesthetic skepticism with which this essay began: "There is not much artistic possibility to be found in caring for a sick friend, enduring an unhappy marriage, performing uncongenial work." There is considerable homiletical possibility, however.

And there is more artistic possibility than Wood might allow. Let me name just three contemporary novelists who find the possibilities of grace, of transcendence, of a kind of saintliness even, in the most ordinary lives: Anne Tyler, Wendell Berry, and Richard Russo. I have no idea how far they act out of any sense of religious vocation, but I do know that in reading them I see just such matters as caring for a sick friend, putting up with a job you don't much like (Russo, *Nobody's Fool*), getting old (Berry, *The Memory of Old Jack*), rejoicing and grieving as the children grow up and grow away (Tyler, *Ladder of Years*), acknowledging and transcending guilt (Tyler, *Saint Maybe*), grieving a death that is both loss and release (Tyler, *Dinner at the Homesick Restaurant*)—I see just such matters as ways in which mercy is not just described but shown. Preachers do not always need to quote such writers, and it is often difficult to do so without recounting elaborate plots, but we can read them to get ideas of how to bring that amazing intersection of the ordinary and the astonishing together.

Barbara Brown Taylor and Gardner Taylor write sermons that are like very good poems; and Denise Levertov and R. S. Thomas write poems that are like very good sermons (not, for me, an insult). Fun as it is to read P. D. James, who is indeed a thoughtful Christian as well as a fine writer, it is also fun to read these others. It would be a huge mistake to imitate them, and probably even to recite their words at length. But it is a gift to learn from them, to love words the way they love words, to remember that preaching is always show-and-tell time, and that showing is at least as important as telling.

Let one instance stand as a sign of hope for novelists and preachers, too. The novel is Anne Tyler's *Breathing Lessons*. It is, of all grace-filled amazements, the story of the sometimes strained love affair between a man and a woman who have been married for twenty-six years, about the surprises and the decisions that can sustain us.

As the novel ends, Maggie comes into the bedroom for the night. Ira, her husband, is sitting up on his side of the bed playing solitaire. Anne Tyler describes Maggie's thoughts in language, that like biblical language, works at two levels all at once. More than one kind of game. More than one kind of trip.

> Maggie spun around and returned to the bed. "O Ira," she said, dropping down beside him, "what are we two going to live for, all the rest of our lives?"
>
> She had dislodged a stack of his cards, but he kindly refrained from straightening them out and instead reached out one arm and drew her in. "There now, sweetheart," he said, and he settled her next to him. Still holding her close, he transferred a four of spades to a five, and Maggie rested her head against his chest and watched. He had arrived at the interesting part of the game by now, she saw. He had passed that early, superficial stage when any number of moves seemed possible, and now his choices were narrower and he had to show real skill and judgment. She felt a little stir of something that came over her like a flush, a sort of inner buoyancy, and she lifted her face to kiss the warm blade of his cheekbone. Then she slipped free and moved to her side of the bed, because tomorrow they had a long car trip to make and she knew she would need a good night's sleep before they started.[17]

That will preach.

Notes

1. Ralph C. Wood, "A Case for P.D. James as a Christian Novelist," *Theology Today* 59 (January 2003):583–84.
2. John Milton, in Merritt Y. Hughes, ed., *John Milton: Complete Poems and Major Prose* (New York: Odyssey, 1957), bk. 1, lines 249–63.
3. Ibid., bk. 3, lines 294–300.
4. From "Sinners in the Hands of an Angry God," in Wilson H. Kimnach, Kenneth P. Minkema, and Douglas A. Sweeney, *The Sermons of Jonathan Edwards: A Reader* (New Haven, Conn., and London: Yale University Press, 1999), 58.
5. From "The Pleasantness of Religion," in Kimnach, Minkema, and Sweeney, *The Sermons of Jonathan Edwards*, 24. Notice that when he wants to draw delight Edwards draws in biblical imagery, not just propositional claims.
6. Harry Emerson Fosdick, "The Conquest of Fear," sermon in *The Hope of the World: Twenty-five Sermons on Christianity Today* (New York and London: Harper and Row, 1933), 59. The sermon is pp. 59–68. When Fosdick does deal with more than one pastoral or social problem, he brings them together under a larger rubric or theme: "Keeping One's Footing in a Slippery Time" or "Six Ways to Tell Right from Wrong," both in this same volume.
7. Harry Emerson Fosdick, "Dare We Break the Vicious Circle of Fighting Evil with Evil?" A Sermon Preached at the Riverside Church, February 19, 1939 (separate printing), 10.

8. Ibid., 22.

9. See George J. Becker, *Realism in Modern Literature* (New York: Ungar, 1980).

10. Janet Maslin in the *New York Times*, accessed online.

11. Erich Auerbach, *Mimesis: The Representation of Reality in Western Literature*, trans. Willard R. Trask (Princeton, N.J.: Princeton University Press, 1953), 22–23.

12. Ibid., 11.

13. Robert Frost, "To the Thawing Wind" and "Stopping by Woods on a Snowy Evening," in *The Poetry of Robert Frost* (New York: Henry Holt, 1969), 11, 224.

14. See Jack Miles, *God: A Biography* (New York: Vintage, 1996).

15. There is another way in which we may need to honor the biblical texts, and that is by paying attention to apocalyptic. In the Bible on those occasions when the writer does recite the laundry list of evils, the laundry list is usually elaborated in images drawn from Old Testament prophecy and traditional apocalyptic, and the description of redemption is as elaborate as the description of distress. We may need a richer ability to claim the Bible's hope of cosmic redemption before we are able to preach effectively on cosmic woes.

16. Frederick Buechner, *Telling Secrets* (San Francisco: HarperSanFrancisco, 1991), 2–3.

17. Anne Tyler, *Breathing Lessons* (New York: Alfred A. Knopf, 1988), 326–27.

Chapter Two

A Fearful Pulpit, a Wayward Land

David Buttrick

osdick's famous article "What Is the Matter with Preaching?" appeared in 1928, at a time when people seemed to care about preaching. But in 1929 the stock market collapsed and hard reality edged into the American soul. Since then times have changed. People care about films, rock bands, first-strike capability, good sex, and any number of other weighty matters. Preaching is not high on anyone's list of public concerns—not even among the clergy! But a "What is the matter with" essay could tumble into carping criticism, so, temporarily, we'll turn Fosdick's title inside out: "What is the *usefulness* of preaching?" Let us begin with a minimal defense of the pulpit.

I

In any age, the virtue of religious speaking is that it names God into human consciousness. Even if such preaching is neither biblically nor theologically adept, at least preaching names God. Thus, if nothing else, God is kept in the social vocabulary. Our contemporary culture is fabricated out of language (in all its manifold forms). A large share of such language is wielded by advertising agencies, public-relations people, church-growth types, and, of late, presidential press secretaries. Such persons speak out of self-interest, or if not self-interest, certainly the interests of a particular corporate group. Language can be many things. Obviously language can be a gift with no strings attached, an act of love, or, as easily, an attempt to control our thoughts, social attitudes, product preferences, and political choices. Bad preaching can also seek to coerce faith, and thus misrepresent the God who sets people free. But, please notice, even bad preaching names God. Therefore, though naming God may seem minimal, it is nonetheless the basic urgency of religious speaking.

Of course, when preaching happens in the context of worship not only is God named into human consciousness, but selves along with others bow before God, or stand to praise God; they sing hymns, they recite creeds, they pray unison prayers, they may even relate to other worshipers with a somewhat tepid handshake version of the liturgical "kiss of peace." If worship is practiced in its proper fullness, they also will share food in a rather peculiar banquet: bread as basic human foodstuff, wine as a celebrative gift. The bodily postures, the interrelating, the voicing of faith all contribute to the reality of the named God. They define us before God and in relationship to others who are also bowing, standing, singing, feasting. Actually, speaking God is an everywhere sport. God can be mentioned in political rallies, union meetings, football games, as well as those rare moments of corporate ethical deciding. But "church" is reconstituted regularly by naming God in the context of public worship. So, at the outset, let us not disparage preaching. Preaching names God into human consciousness. In-church preaching names God so as to define and sustain churches as "people of God."

II

As for what is the *matter* with preaching today, the topic would seem to involve us in historical reflection and, perhaps, in some prescriptive dreaming.[1] Suppose we begin by drifting back into the twentieth century, which as we all know was not so long ago, and then conclude with a look to the future of Christian preaching.

The century began with homiletic fragmentation: social gospel preaching, "new school" revivalism, and "old school" orthodoxy—all of which were inherited from the nineteenth century. But after the first quarter of the century, after World War I and a "Great Depression," we saw the rise of neoorthodoxy. Most mainline preachers today have been educated under the auspices of neoorthodoxy; perhaps most still are. In Protestant seminaries neoorthodoxy involved a return to Pauline biblical faith and Augustinian theology in both Lutheran and Reformed versions. After midcentury, Barthian "biblical theology" became the primary exponent of the neoorthodox tradition. We might note, however, that an extreme "Word of God" theology, demoting *analogia entis* (analogy of being) as well as "natural theology," could easily become remote or turn crypto-fundamentalist. Under the aegis of neoorthodoxy, the *basileia* (or "empire of God") preaching of Jesus tended to disappear. In mid-twentieth century, "kingdom of God" was often dismissed as a nineteenth-century liberal invention.[2]

So what about preaching in the second half of the twentieth century? Elsewhere I have argued that preaching moved in three different directions, all transformations of nineteenth-century orientations: "biblical preaching," proposed earlier in the century by P. T. Forsyth, a largely Barthian enterprise[3]; "therapeutic personalism," in part a result of Fosdick's "project method"; and "social vision" preaching, by Martin Luther King Jr. and Malcolm X. Toward the end of the century we might need to add a fourth concern, namely, "preaching the institution," perhaps a product of "church management" literature, or simply a reaction to the numerical decline of mainline congregations. Let us rehearse these three main options.

Biblical Preaching

If we look at the homiletic literature from midcentury on, it was predominantly concerned with preaching biblical pericopes. Topical preaching was shunned, as well as sermons launched from single-verse topical pretexts. We championed "biblical preaching." During the '60s and '70s, such literature was written by biblical scholars and theologians, as well as by homileticians.[4] Behind the rise of the biblical theology movement were certain assumptions, namely, an emphasis on Bible to the neglect of nature and experience. Karl Barth went so far as to argue the sermon should be nothing more than "the involuntary lip movement of one who is reading" Scripture.[5] Because most homileticians appear to be Barthian, the pulpit is still under the sway of the movement. Sermons are apt to be backward looking, hankering for the good old days when God acted in history or, to be exact, in "our story," namely, the Bible. As a result, many sermons begin with historical background then seek to bridge time and speak now—a past-tense God for present-tense people. There is little conviction that now, right now, God could speak to us through sermons. For Martin Luther, *preaching* was the Word of God. Thus the Bible was also Word of God *insofar as it contained preaching*, a declaration of the gospel message. But Barth, in line with Calvinism, announced enigmatically that "Scripture is recognized as the Word of God because it *is* the Word of God,"[6] and then proceeded to assess preaching on the basis of whether it was properly biblical. Preachers, said Barth, "must accept the necessity of expounding the Book and *nothing* else."[7]

Biblical preaching was supported in the '70s by a turn toward the liturgical lectionary. Most lectionaries worked from Vatican proposals, modified by skipping some un-Protestant Marian feasts as well as most saints' days. Gradually a "Common Lectionary" formed, with the result that a great many clergy now preach the lectionary somewhat compulsively.[8] Ministers no longer have to research texts on their own; instead they can subscribe to lectionary aids, exegetical and homiletical. More and more ministers are chasing predesigned lectionary sermons (sometimes downloaded from the Internet). The excitement of discovering meaning through texts as well as the exhilaration of homiletic craft is thus seldom experienced. Still more, the regimented compulsion of lectionary preaching seems to offer an out for clergy who would rather not address the sociopolitical world in which we live. Liturgical churches have lived with lectionaries for centuries; their clergy understand that the lectionary isn't law, and that the pulpit can preach beyond required readings, with theological or prophetic purpose. But churches without a long-term lectionary tradition can become slavishly bound to lections, and what's more enjoy the bondage. Lectionaries are useful; they keep the Bible before the churches. But a fixed schedule of readings, even when designed to serve the church year, may pose some problems.

In England years ago, someone manufactured a box of scrolled Bible verses. The box had thirty-one compartments, and in each was a little scroll to be opened day by day a month at a time, offering persons direct messages from God. The practice was obviously nonsense, a form of pious magic. Inasmuch as the box came with only one set of favorite verses, the pious reader soon grew weary of the worn-out words of God. Question: Is lectionary preaching all that different? Must every sermon begin with a biblical passage? Do we not preach from theological concern? Can we not instruct from the liturgy? Are we not called to address the social world prophetically, sometimes using quite different texts than those assigned, or no texts! Certainly we preachers preach knee-deep in grace, but remember, grace is free and given to serve God and neighbors with the freedom of the gospel message.

Therapeutic Preaching

The other dominant mode of preaching since the '50s can be described as "pastoral" or "therapeutic." Though Harry Emerson Fosdick may have emerged from a social gospel background, his "project method" clearly moved preaching in the direction of personal pastoral care. As we've seen in the *Harper's* essay, Fosdick was blunt: "There is nothing that people are so interested in as themselves, their own problems, and the way to solve them." For Fosdick, the test of a good sermon was "how many individuals wish to see the preacher alone" for counseling. Even if a preacher speaks to hundreds, Fosdick claimed, the preacher "speaks to them as individuals and is still a personal counselor."[9] Fosdick himself did speak out on public issues, particularly as he was prompted by his own pacifism; nonetheless, following Fosdick most American sermons have been aimed at individual selves in their self-awareness. During the last half of the twentieth century, American preaching gave in to "the triumph of the therapeutic." The result: two problems.

The first I addressed elsewhere:

> Preaching to personal, psychological problems isn't necessarily bad—most of us need all the help we can get—but it can be dangerous. Question: Is God, the holy God of Israel, nothing more than a free therapist for individual problems? . . . The problem with therapeutic preaching is not that it's bad—no, it is often tender and helpful—but it may limit theological meaning and it can excuse our silence about public affairs, which is exactly what has been happening in most mainline pulpits—a huge silence about public affairs. Many, if not most American pulpits, following Fosdick and fanned by the existentialist fifties, have tumbled into a narrow personalism. As a result, the God the pulpit announces is a God no larger than the reflection of our psychological needs, a God who has no concern for social justice. To put it bluntly, therapy is OK as long as you don't mind living with Pharaohs![10]

Second, the individual focus of therapeutic preaching is problematic. The pulpit appears to be preoccupied with what might be termed a one-to-one self in one-to-one relationships or the self in one-to-one internal dialogue. The problem with such an approach is that the pulpit may end up addressing an *abstraction;* there may be no such thing as a one-to-one self! If personal preaching aims at a self-without-a-world, then social gospel preaching regards a world-without-a-self, and both are obvious unrealities. As playwright Tony Kushner has observed, "The smallest divisible human unit is two people, not one; one is a fiction."[11] We are never one, even when we are alone, but always a complex self wound around with webs of relationship.

We have described two trends of twentieth-century preaching: biblical and therapeutic preaching. I suspect they have merged, biblical positivism addressing subjective personalism. If Barth insisted on "the necessity of expounding the Book and *nothing else*" (emphasis added), perhaps Fosdick added an extra piece of advice: "to individual felt needs." Has preaching the Bible replaced preaching the gospel? Has personal therapy displaced the redemptive purposes of God? The most obvious judgment on American preaching in recent times has been the failure to take on the White House over the prospect of a war with Iraq. One of the signs carried in the huge peace march on Washington, D.C., in February 2003 read, "Where are the churches?" Yes, there were individual Christians marching, and a few denominational statements made, but the silence of local pulpits on the administration's eagerness for war was deafening. Was the silence prompted by predominantly Republican congregations in mainline churches? Probably. Or does the mix of biblical lections and personal-need preaching bypass public issues? Barth may have helped to draft the Barmen Declaration, but Barthian preaching tempered by therapeutic concern has somehow dodged national policy. The American pulpit is thereby condemned.

Black Preaching

The trends we have noted apply mostly to white preaching in middle-class white congregations. Inasmuch as such locations will constitute a minority report in three or four decades when America will be predominantly black and Spanish speaking, obviously my analysis is skewed. Black preaching, such as the sermons of M. L. King Jr preaching Christianity and Malcolm X preaching Islam, has had huge social impact, not only in our land, but all over the world. Moreover, black pulpits have had more than a share of great preachers, from Richard Allen, son of a slave, to Gardner Taylor, the "Dean of Black Preachers" today.[12] They have brought the gospel message to African American congregations. Then suddenly in the last half of the twentieth century, black preaching emerged to reach a wider public audience. Henry Mitchell, a remarkable homiletician, has described the genre. In addition to Gardner Taylor, stunning preachers filled American black pulpits during the decades: Howard Thurman, Samuel Proctor, J. Alfred Smith Sr., and many, many others; plus splendid women preachers such as Katie Cannon, Vasti Murphy McKenzie, and Carolyn Ann Knight. There are so many grand black preachers any listing would overcrowd a page. Of course, to be honest, there are inadequate black preachers as there are inadequate white preachers, but all things considered, since 1960 the best preaching in America has been happening in African American settings.

Please note, black preachers preach the Bible and, in fact, are biblically conservative. Having taught in both black and predominantly white theological schools, I can testify that African American students generally know more Bible than white students, often by heart. What's more, many black preachers are delighted by Karl Barth's conviction that the biblical Word of God is inevitably countercultural. So why hasn't the African American pulpit tumbled into a cryptofundamentalist biblicism?

There seem to be at least two reasons: First, black preaching hears the Bible as story. Notice the verb "hears." Slave religion passed along the Bible as an unfolding story, and not as a written-down book. If the Bible is an objective written-down history, then questions of fact arise to keep both fundamentalist and liberal scholars busy. But questions of literal history fade when a good story is told. So what if Matthew misquotes some prophets, or Mark gets confused over geography? The storyteller doesn't trouble with trivia; no, the storyteller is eager to tell a good, dramatic, unforgettable story and above all bring out meaning, namely, the mystery of the living God with us. But the story that the Bible tells is a story of God and all sinning humanity; it is not a limited "our story" of the church. No wonder black preaching gives meaning to the whole human enterprise. If the Bible is a preached, oral story the tendency to idolatrous biblicism is reduced.

Second, black preaching interprets the Bible within a hermeneutic of freedom. Because the exodus story is paradigmatic and a clue to the nature of God—God is the God who sets people free—black preaching looks to the future, singing, "Oh, Freedom." So the hermeneutic of black preaching celebrates the future promises of God.[13] No wonder black preaching giggles over the pretensions of white society, and ends almost every sermon in celebration.[14] The black pulpit knows what Jesus knew—the end of the Bible story is beyond the Bible when, in an empire of God, we will gather for the biggest fish-fry party anyone can imagine. Freedom! The gospel message of God's redemptive promises is the context in which the Bible is understood. Thus black preaching does not end up announcing a once-upon-a-time biblical God and then trying to bridge to the twenty-first century. No, African American preachers, speaking between exodus and ultimate freedom, announce a present-tense liberating gospel.

What about Fosdick's "project method" in black churches? African American preaching addresses a common consciousness, and therefore Fosdick's implicit individualism never took hold. After all, black congregations share a common reality, blackness in a racist society, and therefore common oppression. Preachers address black congregations as one, sometimes as a personified one, but always as one unified consciousness. The phrase "black identity" defines the audience for preaching. These days white congregations seem to celebrate their individual disunity; pluralism is a boast. But if God addresses us through preaching, the address of God constitutes us as one people. Will social fragmentation emerge as the black middle class multiplies? Perhaps. Some "buppie" churches seem to be speaking individual therapy. But as of now, social oppressions have created a special solidarity in black congregations. Still, beyond unity in oppression, black preaching with its exodus emphasis and freedom eschatology speaks to a liberated people as one people. Thus, black preaching reads biblical texts correctly, for the Bible speaks to a corporate reality.

Have all black churches retained a prophetic edge? Somewhat. Certainly, the theology of ministerial "call" is understood within prophetic models—God called Moses, Isaiah, Jeremiah, Amos, and others. Thus God is calling black preachers to speak words of God to God's people. What's more, black preachers have grasped the Hebrew Bible as a story of God's interaction—Word to words—with God's recalcitrant people. So, for the most part, black preachers speak out, helping congregations see themselves as both separate from and critical of establishment social patterns. Most black churches are opposing America's war plans, for, after all, black eschatology envisions "shalom." Will the prophetic edge ebb as black churches become more monied? Possibly, for as we all know America is hopelessly corrupted by cash.

III

Now let us ask about the future of preaching in America. America is a reactionary land. We have cash and we have power and we have not shown much impulse to share either. Though many Americans begrudge foreign aid, if truth is told it only represents about a single percent of the national budget. The world is hungry, often impoverished, and we have not been generous. What's more, our involvement in worldwide economic affairs seems guaranteed to keep poor lands in their poverty. Our domestic policies are no more admirable. In the United States the rich have been getting richer and the poor multiplying. We have no national health care for all citizens. Our public schools are underfunded, our welfare programs miniscule, unsupported by adequate child-care programs. Do our pulpits address such issues? Generally, no. But preaching that does not build concern for the human common good is downright unsatisfactory, if not wicked.[15] How has the pulpit tumbled into irrelevancy? How has the pulpit lost "public voice"? Let us turn and ask what can be done. I have four suggestions.

Suggestion one: *Preaching will have to have an eye for what the Bible calls "principalities and powers."* Once more we must be alert to the transsocial images, ideas, and institutions that can hold human minds captive. To paraphrase Ephesians 6:12: We wrestle not with personal problems alone, but "against the principalities, against the powers, against the cosmocrats of this present darkness, against unseen forces in high places." Can Americans see that we are in bondage, trapped within shibboleths and systems of our own invention? Suppose as a preacher you wish to urge your congregation to lead simple lives in solidarity with the poor, will you even be able to get through to your people? Our fantasies are shaped by advertising—the gold-knobbed stereo, a "four-on-the-floor" sports car, the fire-lit family room clipped from *Better Homes and Gardens*. Such images are bolstered by slogan phrases—"high standard of living," "free economy," "the good life." The principalities and powers hold us in sway, generating not merely our economic fantasies, but our prejudices as well—our systemic racism and obvious sexism, our insular nationalism, not to mention our absurd "We're number one" military buildups—they are all sustained by the "powers that be."

We have not figured out how to preach to the "principalities and powers." Instead we have hawked personal salvation. We have pictured sin as an inward fault that shows up in our fears and guilts and anxieties; to us, sin is a matter of the heart. We have told congregations that they can be new people inside themselves and enjoy "peace with God" and, as a byproduct, happiness. Thus, they can accept themselves and even sport a touch of deserved self-esteem. All they have to do is to believe in Jesus. Inasmuch as we describe faith as an inner disposition, the whole saving work of God happens *unseen*, in the heart. In effect, we have reinstated a gnostic heresy! Jesus can save our inner selves, but when it comes to the social order he is not much use. For the social order we will have to find some other savior, usually an "ism," or at least a political loyalty. The tragedy in American Protestantism is that we have a whole nation full of born-again Jesus people who nevertheless support appalling social policies—including first-strike action in Iraq! The therapeutic pulpit has preached Jesus as a half-savior: he brings relief to the psychologically burdened heart, but as for the "principalities and powers," he is uninvolved or even impotent.

Suggestion two: *If we are going to speak of social salvation, once more we will have to preach the preaching of Jesus, namely, the coming of the empire of God.*

In a neoorthodox season, talk of the *basileia* of God is suspect; good heavens, who wants to be labeled a lightweight, theological liberal. But according to Scripture, Jesus came preaching, "The time is up, the empire of God is on the way; repent and believe the good news." We have been telling people to "repent and believe" and get right with God, but we have dropped the reason for repentance, namely, the coming of God's new social order. The notion of God's promised social order animates the whole Bible from the call of Abram to the vision of Isaiah to the preaching of Jesus to the final chapters of Revelation. But, though biblical, we have largely skipped the preaching of Jesus for a message about Jesus, our patented heart savior. Of late, America has been hankering for the past—old-time free enterprise, old-time states' rights; old-time, down-home, oaken-bucket religion—and quite afraid of social change. If you have achieved a pleasant middle-class status, you're not eager for social change. If you have adjusted to middle-class life, your self-image, and inward well-being, you fear psychological change almost as much. The Beatitudes sing a song of God's promises; the poor will be lifted up, the hungry fed, the weepers laugh, the peacemakers triumph. The poor, the impotent, the hungry—mostly they live beyond us in the wide, hurt world. Maybe we care a little, but not enough to vote for any diminishing of our all-American prosperity. No wonder we'd rather not preach the social promises of God, even though they are assuredly biblical.

The gospel Jesus preached, the coming of God's new order, gives meaning to the human world. Right now, worldwide, we are facing up to meaninglessness. The metanarratives within which people view their lives have disappeared; *Pilgrim's Progress* has given way to *Psychology Today*. As a result most people now view their lives as a series of short-term objectives: I will finish school, I will get laid, I will buy a car, I will get a job, I will be married, I will have children, I will start an IRA. In turn, these unfolding purposes are urged by an avaricious advertising industry. But if we are asked to articulate some overall meaning to our lives, well, we haven't a clue! The loss of meaning has been documented as a worldwide catastrophe. And a gospel—I am tempted to say, a heretical gospel—of "personal salvation" is a shabby substitute. No, for life to have meaning we must have some vision of the ultimate purposes of God; what has God got in mind for the whole human enterprise? The idea of the empire of God visualizes end-term purposes of God. Because God is, and is involved with us in shaping a human future, we can assume that God is trying to love us toward some improvisational version of the empire of God. Thus we are able to venture moral notions: for example, that God desires peace, not armed conflict; that God desires the hungry be fed and the poor given a share of prosperity. The biblical image of God's realm defines our shared human calling under God as well as documenting various forms of recalcitrant disobedience.[16] If giving meaning to life is *the* task of preaching, and surely it is, then once more we must echo the preaching of Jesus in our pulpits.

Suggestion three: *If we preach God's social vision, we will invoke the presence of God. Without social eschatology there is no presence of God.* We have alluded to Tony Kushner's grand play, *Angels in America.* In the drama, angels actually arrive. They turn out to be ancient figures toting around a whopping big book. They explain that they are not sure when or if God will be returning to America again, but that meanwhile they will go by The Book! Some reviewers had difficulty identifying the "angels," but we should have no trouble—they are us. Ever since the late '50s, we have not exactly been gripped by a strong social sense of the presence of God, but meanwhile we have been obsessed with The Book. We have denied "general revelation," and desacralized the natural world. Instead, we have spoken of God's revelation in history, singularly in the figure of Jesus the Christ, all of which we find wrapped up in The Book. We have been telling congregations about a past-tense God, who once was; like the fuddled "angels," we clutch The Book. Of course, the Judeo-Christian tradition does testify that God was with Israel, and in Christian writing that God was related singularly to Jesus of Nazareth, but such testimony does not necessarily produce a sense of presence. Without a gospel that includes the eschatological future of God, presence is always uncertain. No wonder that after a century of biblical preaching people in church and out seem to be seeking a more immediate experience of God via various forms of "spirituality," some helpful, some misleading. Ultimately, God's awesome presence can be affirmed only by looking to the future of God, a God whom we have heard of in the past—the one eternal God, "from everlasting to everlasting."

Maybe we should scuttle the "mighty acts of God in history" model and, in turn, speak of a God who interfaces humanity in multiple ways through the social symbols, images, arts, witnesses that shape us in faith, right now. Above all, let us seek to restore a public awareness of God by naming the influence of God on our common lives, and by tracing, as we are able, the mysterious movements of grace among us. God is Merciful Consciousness, conscious of us; "in him we live and move and have our being" (Acts 17:28). Biblical theology has tumbled into a kind of scriptural arrogance; as a result, most ministers preach the Bible's past-tense God, but have lost track of theological thoughtfulness. Originally, just as philosophy and rhetoric were allied, theology and homiletics also walked arm in arm.[17] The alliance of homiletic practice and biblical theology is something newer than we know. Now, as the biblical theology movement is ebbing, we are beginning to question: Is preaching the Bible the same thing as preaching the gospel? The task of preaching is to declare the gospel from a deep theological understanding of our faith.

Suggestion four: *If we preach God's social vision, preaching will lead us to eucharistic celebration.* The individualism of Free Church Protestant preaching obviously has undercut eucharistic celebration. In a recent article, Robert Bellah explains that though he used to single out Puritan Anne Hutchinson as the first prototypical American Protestant, now he nominates Roger Williams, whom he labels a moral genius but "a sociological catastrophe." Williams founded the first Baptist Church in Rhode Island, but left it for a smaller, purer one. Finally, according to Bellah, finding the second congregation inadequate, "Williams founded a church that consisted only of himself, his wife and one other person. One wonders how he stood even those two." The verdict, according to Bellah: Williams is an example of "what happens when the individual is not balanced by any sense of the whole or concern for the common good."[18] Free Church preaching tends to suppose that the end of the gospel message is the inner faith and moral purity of a converted individual, but properly the fulfillment of the gospel message is incorporation in Eucharist.[19] Eucharist is social symbol of God's new humanity in the midst of our sin-wearied world. The Supper can and should be an enacted symbol of the promised empire of God.

During the twentieth century, as with preaching, liturgical historians often seemed to be looking backward to ancient Hippolytus as a model of practice, though he was a rather reactionary guide. Committees drafting eucharistic prayers seemed compulsively into anamnesis, but startlingly short of end-term language for the purposes of God. As neoorthodoxy had, they seemed to sidestep allusions to the *basileia* of God. But, must we not suppose that the earliest feasts, though remembering the whole story of God's graciousness, and reciting the life, death, and resurrection of Jesus, were also proleptic celebrations of the promised "kingdom." If we preach the preaching of Jesus, namely, news of *basileia*, perhaps our preaching will restore the glad theme of God's future in eucharistic celebration.

IV

Authority for preaching is not conferred by the Bible, or by the church, or by some test of "effectiveness." Paul, the apostle, was evidently a wretched preacher. No, preaching is prompted by the living God who reaches toward us all redemptively through words and images and social symbols, our memories, and our hopes. Preaching does not merely testify to God's past-tense redemptive actions, but *participates in God's redemptive purposes now:*

> True preaching is not therapy or church management or a reiteration of the Bible; true preaching is positively scary! Preachers are people who dare a dangerous work; they name God in the world. So preaching is ultimately an act of courage. We speak in the strange presence-in-absence of God, as a human being to human beings, and tremble; fortunately, according to the promises of God, free fine preaching is always graceful—that is, *grace* full.[20]

Nowadays, American preaching may find renewal by turning around and once more looking ahead to the gospel promises of God.

Notes

1. See my Disciples Lectureship in which I revisited Fosdick's question fifteen years ago: "Preaching in an *Un*brave New World," *The Spire* 13 (Summer/Fall 1988): 1.
2. In keeping with the Jesus Seminar, I prefer to render "kingdom of God" as "empire of God." The translation has two advantages in our North American context: (1) it avoids the sexism of *king*dom, as well as fairy-tale associations prompted by kings and kingdoms; and (2) it matches the term "Roman Empire." Both Niebuhrs viewed "kingdom of God" notions with suspicion. In particular, see H. Richard Niebuhr, *The Kingdom of God in America* (New York: Harper and Row, 1937).
3. See my review essay, "P. T. Forsyth: The Man, the Preacher's Theologian, Prophet for the Twentieth Century," *Princeton Seminary Bulletin* 6 (1985): 231–34.
4. See, for example, theologians: Dietrich Ritschl, *A Theology of Proclamation* (Richmond: John Knox, 1960) and J. J. Von Allmen, *Proclamation and Congregation* (Richmond: John Knox, 1962); biblical scholars: Leander Keck, *The Bible in the Pulpit: The Renewal of Biblical Preaching* (Nashville: Abingdon, 1978) and Ernest Best, *From Text to Sermon: Responsible Use of the New Testament in Preaching* (Atlanta: John Knox, 1978). Earlier, Donald G. Miller, biblical scholar and homiletician, wrote two well-read works, *Fire in Thy Mouth* (1954) and *The Way to Biblical Preaching* (1957), both published by Abingdon.
5. Karl Barth, *Homiletics*, trans. Geoffrey W. Bromiley and Donald E. Daniels (Louisville, Ky.: Westminster/John Knox, 1991), 76. The backwash of the biblical theology movement is still with us, though its basic assumptions have been brutally challenged. See, for instance, James Barr, "Revelation through History in the Old Testament and in Modern

Theology," in Martin E. Marty and Dean G. Pearlman, eds., *New Theology* (New York: Macmillan, 1964), 60–74.

6. Karl Barth, *Church Dogmatics* I/2, trans. G. T. Thompson and Harold Knight (Edinburgh: T. and T. Clark, 1956), 537.

7. Karl Barth, *The Preaching of the Gospel*, trans. B. E. Hooke (Philadelphia: Westminster, 1963), 43. (Emphasis added.)

8. See my article "Preaching the Lectionary: Two Cheers and Some Questions," *Reformed Liturgy and Music* 28 (Spring 1994): 77–81.

9. Harry Emerson Fosdick, "Personal Counseling and Preaching," *Pastoral Psychology* 3 (March 1952); reprinted in Lionel Crocker, ed., *Harry Emerson Fosdick's Art of Preaching* (Springfield, Ill.: Charles C. Thomas Publisher, Ltd., 1971), 55.

10. David Buttrick, "*Un*brave New World," 12.

11. Tony Kushner, *Angels in America: A Gay Fantasia on National Themes*, pt. 2, *Perestroika* (New York: Theatre Communications Group, 1994), 158. On the interhuman, see Edward Farley, *Good and Evil: Interpreting the Human Condition* (Minneapolis: Fortress, 1990), chap. 12.

12. For a brief history of African American preaching, Charles V. Hamilton, *The Black Preacher in America* (New York: Morrow, 1972). For an excellent bibliography on the black preaching tradition, see Robert R. Howard, "African American Preaching: A Bibliography," pt. 1, *Homiletic* 23 (Winter 1998): 25–30; pt. 2, *Homiletic* 26 (Summer 2001):1–4. On black preaching, the literature is huge, but see Cleophus J. LaRue, *The Heart of Black Preaching* (Louisville, Ky.: Westminster John Knox, 2000).

13. See Susan L. Bond, "To Hear the Angels' Wings: Apocalyptic Language and the Formation of Moral Community with Reference to the Sermons of Gardner C. Taylor" (Ph.D. diss., Vanderbilt University, 1996).

14. On the countercultural giggle in African American preaching, see my chapter "Laughing with the Gospel," in *Sharing Heaven's Music: Essays on Christian Preaching in Honor of James Earl Massey*, ed. Barry L. Callen (Nashville: Abingdon, 1995). On celebration, see Henry H. Mitchell, *Celebration and Experience in Preaching* (Nashville: Abingdon, 1990).

15. See Robert N. Bellah et al., *The Good Society* (New York: Alfred A. Knopf, 1991), chap. 6, "The Public Church."

16. See David Buttrick, *Preaching the New and the Now* (Louisville, Ky.: Westminster John Knox, 1998), a book that studies what it means to preach the "kingdom of God."

17. For the most comprehensive tracing of the relation between homiletics and theology, see Teresa Lockhart Stricklen, "Preaching and Theology in Light of Theological Education: The Early History of a Troubled Marriage, or, What Went Wrong and How" (Ph.D. diss., Vanderbilt University, 2001).

18. Robert N. Bellah, "Religion and the Shape of National Culture," *America*, July 31, 1999, 9–14.

19. James Nelson Fitzgerald, "Weaving the Rope of Sand: Separation of the Proclamation of the Word and the Celebration of the Eucharist in the Church of the Nazarene" (Ph.D. diss., Vanderbilt University, 1999).

20. Buttrick, "*Un*brave New World," 14.

Chapter Three

A Lover's Quarrel with Preaching

Ernest T. Campbell

Years ago I was advised always to ask three questions when reviewing books: What is the author trying to do? Did she/he do it well? Was it worth doing? The first two of these questions hold out the hope for some objectivity. An author's *purpose* can be ascertained. An author's *proficiency* can be assessed. But the third question raises the specter of subjective, even subversive personal judgment: was it worth doing? The reviewer's own stance and range of beliefs will come into play.

Answers to the question, What's the matter with preaching today? will probably reveal as much about each respondent as it does about the preaching art per se. Someone who harbors a fierce resistance to "feel-good pop psychology" efforts in the pulpit will never pronounce a sermon good that comes from a "positive thinking" pulpit. On the other hand, those who hold that "In a democracy religion is necessary to the success of national effort" (a motto posted in the Pentagon years ago by a chaplains group) will not likely pronounce a sermon good that hammers away at economic inequities in the land, racism, warmongering, capital punishment, or the rights of the homeless. Amos and Jeremiah have had their day! So some claim, "If you cannot say anything positive about America, don't say anything. Politics and religion don't mix!"

Thus, for me honest confession is the place to start. One has to own up to a particular theological location before tackling any question about the quality of preaching anywhere. This is where I am coming from:

1. I believe that the Bible is basic to the life of the church, but that the Bible does not have to be taken literally to be taken seriously.

2. I believe that by the action of the Holy Spirit the written Word through the spoken word can become a living word for all who will to hear it.

3. I believe that the worldview of the biblical writers has been rendered obsolete by modern physics and kindred sciences, and that preachers ought not to blink this fact or resist it.

4. I believe that Jesus' *life* is redemptive, not just his death, and that the church through its creeds and modern preachments has obscured this truth by making an unfortunate rush from Bethlehem to Golgotha. We cannot afford to reduce the greatest life ever lived to a mere role in some cosmic drama between the powers of darkness and the power of light.

5. I believe that preaching that fails to address issues of justice and equity in the land mock the prophetic elements of Scripture and cast a silent vote for the status quo. Too many preachers in America have lowered their voices in order to raise their budgets.

6. I believe that while Jesus is the only way for us, he is not necessarily the only way for others. The Great Commission needs to be revisited in a pluralistic age. True, Jesus said, "No one comes to the Father except through me" (John 14:6), but he did not say that the Father comes to no one save through the Son. God is not a prisoner of the incarnation. God can, without mediation, visit whomever God will. It is preposterous and indefensible to deny the possibility of salvation to the billions who share this planet with us but do not share our faith.

Some who have scanned this recital of beliefs will fan other pages of this book in quest of a more theologically friendly mentor. Bless you as you go! But for those who choose to hang on a little longer I want to share some thoughts on preaching from years of *doing* it, *teaching* it, and *hearing* it.

There is discouragement in the ranks. It has become a commonplace in the church to say that preaching isn't what it used to be. Well, *hearing* isn't what it used to be either! The so-called pulpit masters of another age whom we extol, whom we used to listen to by radio, ministered in a vastly different cultural context. Protestant Christianity was the de facto established religion in America in those years. Ministers could speak in public school assemblies up and down the land without a soul to protest. The *New York Times* would review some of Sunday's sermons in their Monday editions. Ball games could not start in New York City until 2 P.M. on Sundays so that churches could have adequate time to do their thing that morning. Sunday movies and Sunday shopping were illegal in many parts of the country. And, most significant of all, there was no television!

I am both old enough and young enough to speak to this dramatic turn of events. In my earliest years out of seminary I remember listening to the *CBS Church of the Air* and NBC's *Sunday Vespers*. It helped a young minister to be paced by the likes of Paul Scherer, Oscar Blackwelder, Theodore Ferris, George Buttrick, John S. Bonnell, Ralph Sockman, Joseph Sizoo, and others. I remember even farther back, to my teen years in New York City, where I had the opportunity each Sunday evening to listen to *The Catholic Hour*, courtesy of NBC, at which time I would be held spellbound by the preaching of Fulton J. Sheen.

To sharpen the point further, in my first major parish in Stroudsburg, Pennsylvania, we were frequently on the air free of charge. And preaching mattered! We had two services each Sunday, morning and evening, and a Bible study on Wednesday nights. I had a fifteen-minute devotional service each Thursday noon that was sponsored by a local bank. We were established! As Archie Bunker would say, "Those were the days."

The first threat to this arrangement came when some villain in a black hat sought to open several of his movie houses on the Lord's Day. There would be a countywide vote on the issue. The churches circled the wagons to defend the traditional Sabbath. Large sums of money were spent by both sides. Sunday movies won!

The second shoe dropped when television came into its own. As a friend of mine likes to point out, with the advent of television fundamentalists could now view in their own homes the movies that their churches had long since opposed. The establishment was slipping, losing its leverage. What preacher was a match for Uncle Miltie? What Sunday evening sermon could compete with *60 Minutes*? And what could be so wrong anyway with families sitting together in their living rooms on a Sunday evening, bonding through a shared interest in some television show?

Impressed by the crashing success of television, some ministers sought to imitate the ways of the new medium. Churches in the round became common. It wasn't good to be seen behind the pulpit as an authority figure. Sauntering up and down the aisles created a better image. Many clergypersons came to see themselves as masters of ceremonies rather than as priests with a duty to order a congregation's worship.

Since television was more visual than oral, ministers were tempted to downplay the unique character of the preached word in favor of "look good, feel good" services. What was forgotten was the fact that nothing the television networks could ever offer could take the place of an ordained pastor standing behind an open Bible in the presence of a believing congregation for the purpose of expounding the truths of the faith. Where ministers held to the efficacy of preaching, congregations thrived. To this day, vacant churches in their quest for a pastor put a high priority on a minister's ability to preach.

The demise of preaching, however, has not come just from without. Our cause has been subverted from within as well. Think, for example, of all the sermons that have been given over to a narrow defense of irrelevant truth. I recall once being part of a three-day seminar on preaching at which a fellow speaker began his first lecture with this astounding statement: "The two gravest threats to the church in America are charismania and charisphobia." What a partisan insight this was! To name an overindulgence in the charismatic and a fear of the charismatic as our foremost dangers is patently absurd. Talk about going to the backwaters of religion for a topic! Such misplaced emphasis gives preaching a bad name.

This brother is but an example to the extreme of the determination of many preachers to defend doctrinal truth of questionable importance. The guy in the back pew who sells underwear in Sears all week is likely to care little about whether we pray *to* Jesus or *through* Jesus; whether the Holy Spirit proceeds from the Father and the Son or from the Father only; whether God predestines all or some or none; whether a literal Jonah was in the belly of a literal fish; whether the Trinity is a fixed entity or a way of describing stages in God's self-disclosure to the world.

All of this may matter, but it cannot matter much. Not in a world where the AIDS virus threatens to wipe out an entire continent; where the world's only superpower is determined to oversee the world by the threat of force; where an economic system seeks to commodify life by putting price tags on everything; where in a city like New York thirty-four thousand homeless persons roam the streets by day and seek shelters by night. Enough already of hairsplitting doctrinal homilies that serve no purpose save that of allowing preachers to sound off on their favorite subjects.

As I see it, there are two kinds of preachers out there. On the one hand we have those who are determined to recover and defend a lost past. Something vital has slipped away. In most cases that which has been lost sight of has to do with one formulation or another of sixteenth-century theology. But to grant finality to one period of theological belief is to be guilty of chronotheism, the worship of a particular time. Has God gone mute since the days of Calvin and Luther? Has the Spirit been on sabbatical since then? By falling down before a sainted past we stand on the verge of ancestor worship.

On the other hand there are those who want to proclaim a living Christ, who is seeking to lead his people into a new and changing world. The Samaritans of old held to the finality and sufficiency of the Pentateuch. The first five books of Moses were enough. The Jews, by contrast, held to an open view of Scripture. Commentary was welcomed, so that ancient truth could be rendered meaningful in the present. Jesus told us that the Spirit would guide us into all truth (John 16:12–13). Good preaching will always strive to keep the future open.

So, from within we have allowed preaching to become a dull defense of the past rather than a daring march into the future. But there's more. We have also fallen too deeply in love with lectionary preaching. When suitable texts are prechosen, some of the magic of homiletical creation is lost. Yes, lectionary preaching has the merit of making preachers confront the biblical text, and textual preaching is always superior to topical. Yes, the lectionary preacher will often meet with other pastors in the area in a common search for meaning. And all of this is good, but there are also outweighing negatives to consider. Let me list a few:

1. The lectionary in its three-year reach covers but a portion of the Bible. How does one justify a system that excludes so much of Scripture?
2. Commitment to the lectionary prevents the preacher from "series preaching." How often these days does one hear about a series of sermons on the Decalogue, the Beatitudes, one-chapter books of the Bible, the journeys of St. Paul, the parables of Jesus? One would be appalled were Shakespeare to be treated in such a hit-and-run manner.
3. The aim of the lectionary is *coverage*, whereas the aim of preaching ought to be *relevance*. If an act of vandalism in Jewish cemeteries has riled up an entire community, are we to expect a sermon that Sunday on the parable of the mustard seed? When a "teachable moment" arrives, we must redeem that opportunity.
4. The number of aids, helps, and "ponies" available now to the working pastor are staggering in their array. The agony that goes with selecting and exegeting a text is replaced by findings of others who have already done the digging. Where is the agony? Where the marks of struggle? The waters of the pool of Bethzatha were salvific only when troubled, says John's Gospel (John 5:1–9). From troubling passages come sermons that make a difference.
5. One can (and should) celebrate the seasons of the Christian year without resorting to lectionary preaching.

I suspect that my feelings about lectionary dependence will not sit well with many whom I should like to count as friends. Before we depart the subject, let me say what I believe about the preaching task. Most critical of all is the choice of theme and subject. Granted, the lectionary reduces the range of possibilities and simplifies the choice. But simpler is not better. A caring pastor should exegete his community and parish to ascertain what word is needed. She should ponder the Scriptures as she knows them in search of the requisite passage. Your digging should be your own. It is better to fail with your own material than to succeed with someone else's. It is called integrity. I doubt that George Buttrick or Paul Scherer or Georgia Harkness ever looked to others before deciding what to preach.

Finally, a word about our failure to connect the "in here" to the "out there." The Christian church is no longer the established religion of the land. We have lost that position of privilege. Good riddance! But we still represent the majority religion in America. How then do we explain the easy way in which Christians in this country have gone along with Madison Avenue by letting their lives be defined by their possessions? "I own, therefore, I am." How explain the nation's support for capital punishment, the free circulation of guns? How explain the massive retreat of the middle class from the inner cities of America, leaving behind demoralized schools, overworked police departments, inadequate health services, and burgeoning welfare rolls?

The abandonment of the city was made possible in part by the reticence of the churches of America. We looked the other way while a dominantly white membership opted for flight to the suburbs. Where were the sermons on the sinfulness of racism and classism? Where the challenge to self-interest and a plea for the common good? We had the numbers to make a difference and we didn't do it! And we are still not doing it! Are we Americans who happen to be Christians, or Christians who happen to be Americans?

Alas, many preachers, far too many, do not regard it as part of their portfolio to address justice issues. By abdicating this field they leave a sizable majority of American citizens without a moral vision. Regressive tax structures, the steady denial of funds for schools and libraries, hanky-panky in the boardrooms of major corporations, the quiet but steady erosion of the planet by profit-driven enterprises, the inability of forty million Americans to obtain health insurance—all of these cry out for homiletical intervention! The fear that by treating such concerns members will leave or vote with their checkbooks should be seen over against the number presently outside the church who are looking to connect with a congregation that shows a social conscience. Surely, Mary's Magnificat (Luke 1:46–55) and Jesus' first sermon in the synagogue at Nazareth (Luke 4:16–30) are enough in themselves to validate the prophetic element in biblical religion.

Many of those who read this book will be pastors in one of our several denominations. I want you to know that I respect your calling and its potential for good in our society. Let me add that I have never met anyone whose preaching improved once that person left the local church. I'm thinking here of ordained men and women who became presbytery executives, seminary professors, bishops, district superintendents, stated clerks, administrators of one sort or another. Some of these may hold their homiletical edge by determination and hard work, but none are likely to improve their preaching. The local church, warts and all, is where it's at! Become vexed if you will by the pettiness of your official board at times, or by the childish ego clashes that you have to deal with in the membership, or the pressures that come down on you from the judicatory to which you belong. But never lose faith in the power of your congregation to make you a better preacher.

Alas, in recent years pastors have been urged to seem more like CEOs than shepherds of the flock. Administrative duties have tended to throw the minister's priorities in disarray. It takes time to be holy. It takes time to study the Word. It takes time to keep up with the scholarship in one's field. It takes time to read beyond one's discipline in quest of material that will fire up the imagination.

Administration can be tamed. Its rigors can be shared, its claims downsized. At times I suspect that one inveighs against administrative duties while at the same time finding in those duties relief from the heavier business of getting down and serious with a text. We can all confess to a tendency to retreat from the mysterious to the manageable. It is easier by far to help the Young Marrieds group plan their breakfast menu than it is to wrestle with a troubling petition of the Lord's Prayer.

George Arthur Buttrick was for me the greatest preacher ever. When he went to the Madison Avenue Presbyterian Church in New York City, he told the people there that they could have everything about him except his mornings. He held to his priorities. After early morning prayers with his staff each day, he repaired to his study. George Buttrick reversed the axiom. He retreated from the manageable to the mysterious. Not a bad pattern. As a result he gave us a book on the parables of Jesus at the age of twenty-eight!

To say that the world is in a state of flux is to thump the obvious. The mighty are shaky in their seats and those of low degree are up and on the march. Old alliances are crumbling and new ones are being formed. Yeast is working the dough of history. For such a time as this have we come to the kingdom. Let this be an incentive to us all: that the mighty Chrysostom, the peerless preacher of his day, did his best pulpit work in the final years of a dying Roman Empire. The best of things in the worst of times. To this we are called!

Chapter Four

Preaching: An Appeal to Memory

Fred B. Craddock

When Harry Emerson Fosdick's "What Is the Matter with Preaching?" appeared in *Harper's Magazine*, I was two months old. I was not impressed; warm milk and a dry diaper were enough for me, thank you. In fact, twenty-two years passed before I read the article. It was on the required reading list for a seminary class, P301. Needless to say, I was impressed. The clarity of his analysis and his skill as a communicator drew me back for a second reading and for several more in the years that followed. Ministers who had wished me "bon voyage" when I left for seminary a few weeks earlier had also warned me about Fosdick and "all those liberals." But Fosdick was required reading; what could I do?

After all these years I continue to learn from the article. However, nothing about it is more impressive than its intended audience. The article did not appear in a clergy journal, but in *Harper's Magazine*! This means that he addressed the general public about preaching. Viewed negatively, he washed our dirty homiletical linen in public. Viewed positively, he spoke to a public still interested in preaching. *Harper's* knew that; otherwise the article would not have been published, even if it was written by Dr. Fosdick of Riverside Church, New York.

Where has that public gone? Perhaps we who preach have driven them away. Certainly some of us act as though that were the case, alternating between self-flagellation and scrambling for a new style, a new medium, a new message that would pull them back. I am not into self-flagellation, but I did my share of scrambling during early pastorates, looking for a homiletical messiah who would provide the magic—anything short of leaping off the pinnacle of the temple. I do not wish to exaggerate here and repent of what is not sin. The pulpit has been greatly helped by new contributions to method from literary studies, hermeneutics, rhetoric, and communication technology. But scrambling is not good; it is anxious, hasty, often careless, and sometimes seduced by the apparent and cosmetic. Even more serious is the tendency of scrambling to overlook solutions and insights close at hand. In that fault may lie a partial answer to the question, What is the matter with preaching?

What, then, is the matter with preaching? Answers come in fragments; we will examine one. If, at its core, preaching is an ongoing conversation between the listeners and the Scriptures, failure to draw on the deep resonances within both listeners and Scripture is one of the more serious oversights. By "deep resonances" I refer to what many thinkers call "memory." Memory is not, however, simply a transaction of deposit and retrieval, as Augustine defined it. This characterization is not to be discarded, for accurate and complete recall is always to be prized and its loss lamented. However, memory is now understood to be much broader and more complex, involving values, identity, relationships, and even hope. We speak of racial memory, bodily memory, personal memory, community memory, national memory. Memory pervades all we are and all we do. John Donne was closer to the current thinking about memory when he said that not the mind and not the will but the memory is the shortest and surest way to God. How far back can one remember? Is it possible that we can remember God? Let's think about it a few minutes.

Why is it that great preaching is characterized by the quality of being a reminder, a reminder of something profoundly true? An answer is immediately available: because the listeners are the already converted, who bring to the sermon prior Christian instruction. Or even if the listeners are not believers, they may stand on much common ground with the speaker. For example, the audience in Jerusalem on the day of Pentecost heard much that was not at all new. After all, as Paul put it, "They are Israelites, and to them belong the adoption, the glory, the covenants, the giving of the law, the worship, and the promises; to them belong the patriarchs, and from them, according to the flesh, comes the Messiah" (Rom. 9:4–5). The audience for Christian missionaries at Athens, however, was quite different. In fact, they said to Paul, "May we know what this new teaching is that you are presenting? It sounds rather strange to us, so we would like to know what it means" (Acts 17: 19–20). And yet, as Paul spoke of the one creator and provider for all people everywhere, he said, "So that they would search for God and perhaps grope for him and find him— though indeed he is not far from each one of us. For 'In him we live and move and have our being'; as even some of your own poets have said, 'For we too are his offspring'" (Acts 17: 27–28). Similarly, Paul and Barnabas had told a crowd in Lystra that God has never anywhere been without a witness in the world (Acts 14:17). These are not simply cases of preachers scrambling for common ground with new and different audiences. Rather, the preachers are assuming that there is in their message something the hearers can not only recognize but welcome as good news. Throughout the history of preaching there are testimonies from first-time hearers who speak of seeming to have heard the message before. The experience is not unlike arriving at a place where you have never been and yet sensing you have been there before. Was Paul saying to his audience in Athens, "Even though you worship at a shrine to an unknown god, I know you recognize what I am saying because it is for this message you have been searching"? At the heart of their not knowing, they know.

Please do not misunderstand me; I am not into self-help and self-fulfilling theology. The trajectory of the Christian faith is from God to us, not from us to God. Salvation is not in searching but in being sought, not in finding but in being found. But is grace undermined if one says that the one who found me is the one I was looking for? Is God's saving initiative taken away if one says that the answer that was given satisfied the question I was asking? Is the bread of heaven less life-giving if received by someone who was hungering for it? I see no reason why our fear of words like "merit" and "works" should blind us to the fact that the search is there, the hunger is there. Of course, we know about Genesis 3: the pride, the unbelief, the disobedience, the loss of Eden, the wandering. But as Ernest Campbell, himself a former pastor of Riverside Church, has been reminding us for years, the Bible does not begin with Genesis 3. To be sure, Genesis 1 and 2 are left in shambles, like a collapsed building, but heaven looks down on the ruins and sees that humanity has gathered enough stones to spell out on the barren land one desperate cry, "Show us God and we will be satisfied." Granted, the churches are not stormed by seekers; the quest is blurred by confusion, disguised by pride, and silenced by fear of rejection. Sin inhibits and distorts the question about God. Press the seeker with too much God talk and one will likely meet resistance, anger, or bad jokes. Do not blame it all on unwillingness; there is also the element of inability to focus the search. Picture someone at midnight standing before an open and well-stocked refrigerator, puzzled: "I'm hungry, but I don't know what I want." So the unvoiced condition of the inquirer before your pulpit may be simply put: "My heart is saying yes to something and I don't know what it is." For this reason, great preaching not only offers an answer but gives voice to the question. The searching listener to your sermon recognizes both the seeking and the finding. The sermon is experienced as new, but not new; it seems a twice-told tale, but the listener does not know why.

And neither does anyone else. Thank goodness preaching does not require that we have the definitive answer, but preaching worth its salt is always haunted by the question and will never cease exploring among the possible answers. If, as we are often being reminded these days, all reading is actually rereading, so all hearing is rehearing. Of course, no message is entirely new; if it were, we could not understand it. Paul acknowledged that in a service of Christian worship even outsiders were able to say, "Amen" (1 Cor. 14:16), but he did not elaborate on the point. We do need to elaborate, however. An answer, admittedly tentative and only partially satisfying, would be welcome. As with so much of Christian theology, a definitive answer is unavailable, but taking a few minutes to recall the principal theories may help us to locate ourselves with some degree of comfort.

First, recall Plato's theory of memory, some forms of which continue to enjoy popularity to this day. Plato believed that our souls began elsewhere and came at birth from the realm of the eternal. The soul, he said, brings with it a recollection of that eternal world and hence is able, on hearing the truth, to resonate with it. This is to say, the truth sounds familiar by reason of that memory. Such a view is used to explain why children are more naturally religious than their parents. Having come fresh from God, children still remember the things of God while their parents have been here too long, mowed too many lawns, and paid too many mortgages to remember very clearly life's whence and whither. However, even those preoccupied with the world and the flesh may cock an ear and be stirred by a sermon passing overhead, much as a goose, having long ago traded the vast skies for a small safe pond, might still be made restless by a faded memory when the giant V-formations honk their way southward. What do you think? I have never been able to fit Plato into the doctrine of creation, but I have long respected this beautiful effort to account for the immense capacities of the human spirit. It is my judgment that we are all the better for having entertained ideas that cannot finally be proven true or false but which, by being treated hospitably for a while, leave us with enlarged and quickened capacities.

Secondly, and perhaps more familiar, is the view that we "recognize" the gospel because there remains in all of us what Rudolf Bultmann called "a faint recollection of Eden." This is not to argue that within human nature is the capacity to remember walking and talking with God in the cool of the day; the fall took care of that. But did nothing survive the fire?

Was everything of Genesis 1–2 demolished? If so, then why does reading those two chapters still stir the heart and wrinkle the brow in a painful push to make the memory say, "Yes, that was home"? Some of us belong to Christian traditions that believe that if you walk around over the charred and smoldering ruins of Genesis 3 you will find a spoon here, a table leg there, a doll's arm over there, and a lamp base near a doorknob. Not much; certainly not enough to encourage even a dream of rebuilding, but maybe enough to kindle hope that there will be a new creation and God will invite us to return.

Many if not most of the preachers I know embrace a third view. According to them (and they are well supplied with the arguments of major theologians), post-fall human beings are totally incapable of hearing a word from God, completely lacking any memory of Eden, however faint, absolutely without any faculty for saying yes to the gospel. Nothing survived the crash of Genesis 3; the word to describe the human condition is depravity. Why, then, preach, if words ricochet off deaf ears and fall unheard to the sanctuary floor? Because God opens ears, because God's prevenient grace makes the heart capable of hearing the gospel, because the same Spirit that inspires the Word works to make the listener receptive. With the Holy Spirit operative at both mouth and ear, all praise belongs to God; human capacities in relation to God are zero. Forget the notion of seeking, of hunger, of longing, of predisposition, of recognition. To be sure, the sermon is a twice-told tale, but only when and where the Spirit of God prepares the listener to make it so.

Others find a more satisfactory explanation for the twice-told nature of preaching in a fourth alternative. This theory enlarges the screen of observation beyond the individual to the human community. Carl Jung, who gave this view its classic expression, concluded after thousands of in-depth sessions with clients in therapy, and after much research into cultures beyond his own observation, that everywhere in the human community there are held in common certain ways of perceiving, apprehending, and defining reality. In what he called the human collective unconscious there exist certain archetypical patterns or images which prescribe the kinds of experiences we have, even though each person's experiences have their own individuality. For example, if I experience fear, the cause and context of that fear are peculiar to me, but the kind of experience fear is conforms to a pattern common to all of us.

Patterns of human responses to life situations do not, as with Plato, have their origin in the eternal realm of the preexisting soul, but rather have emerged in the development of the human race, however diverse and different various societies are on the level of ordinary observation. Out of this pool of the collective unconscious come the capacity and the shape of our responses to words and events. When we hear a message about God's favor toward us, we bring to it not only our own personal histories but also what is called "the memory of the race." In this sense a hearing is a rehearing.

We content ourselves here with only one more attempt to account for sermons' being experienced as memories. This view does not ponder Eden or the fall, it does not assume a collective unconscious, nor does it speculate on what the soul remembers from its life before birth. Here we will think in the world of observable and verifiable realities. Those who lead us in this way of understanding hearing as rehearing do not do so as a way of denying the "spiritual realm." It is, rather, a way of saying that whatever else may be true of our "nature," this too is to be factored in. And what is this view? Simply stated, it is that experience is cumulative, that we are heirs of words and events consciously and unconsciously preserved within and around us, and this fact profoundly affects how and what we hear. There is a layered quality to life, which means that no hearing is really a first hearing. Not only do we all have our personal histories, but we belong to communities with histories. All these communities have their traditions and their texts, and those texts have their subtexts. Carried from generation to generation and from place to place are the stories, the wise sayings, the songs, the rituals, and the embedded values. To belong to a community means to be shaped and defined by these memories even if one has personally rejected some of them along the way. For example, to be a Jew means that one says, "We were in Egypt and God heard our cry," even though one may be a sixteen-year-old living in Vancouver. To be a Christian means that one says, "We were at Golgotha," even though one may be a thirty-year-old living in Santa Fe. So are formed the ears with which we hear, anyone who can remember no farther back than his or her own birth is an orphan.

At some time or other most of us do not like this filtered, this mediated quality of experience. It seems to imply that life for us is secondhand, or diminished, or somehow soiled in the traditioning. And so we are forever fascinated by the "original," the untouched, the unmediated text, the as-he-really-was Lincoln, or Gandhi, or Jesus, the uninterpreted Victoria, or Rachel, or Mary. How zealously we have sought to get behind the Gospels to Jesus, but that Jesus is unavailable to us. That Jesus was not available even to his disciples and friends. In my seminary days we wrote papers not on Luke but Proto-Luke, not on Mark but Ur-Marcus. But there is no

Ur-Wort, no *Himmelbrief*, no message dropped like a meteor from heaven, never before said, never before heard, never before interpreted. Yet we will continue to look and to listen for the original, even though we know that we see with eyes other than our own, we hear with ears other than our own.

As stated above, many of a community's subtexts and much of its memory are received and passed along unconsciously, with little or no interest in sources or the genealogy of ideas. Note the following examples of comments made by persons who had no idea that the language in each case came from the biblical tradition: "I wash my hands of the whole affair," said the outgoing chairman of a social action committee; "I saw the handwriting on the wall," responded the CEO of a large firm to a question about his taking early retirement; "There goes the lamb to the slaughter," commented a sportscaster as a football team took the field. In a culture remarkably ignorant of the Bible, words and phrases from Scripture linger in the language of persons one or two or three generations removed from serious engagement with Jewish or Christian traditions. Likewise, old tunes are whistled and hummed by persons unaware of how they came to lodge in their minds. But those old tunes affect how they feel and think in ways too subtle to trace. Sometimes a new community will borrow a memory from an older community and never return it. It comes to function so helpfully and naturally that the community forgets it was not originally its own. The church borrowed Abraham and Sarah from Israel because the young congregations had no grandparents of their own.

Not that it is always necessary or important to remember what is borrowed or inherited, or from whom. Let the preacher not lament being unable to remember much of what is read and heard. The compost of one's mind may contribute more to effective preaching than what is preserved on note cards. We have learned from therapists how powerful are the unconscious influences, more powerful than the conscious factors that affect behavior, attitudes, and relationships. In fact, if an unconscious "memory" can be brought to the level of consciousness, then it loses much of its power, because now it can be named, identified, and dealt with. On a larger scale, these same factors are operative when one country takes over another. To establish order and prevent revolution, the aggressor seeks to alter the memory of the vanquished country. Styles of dress, holidays, foods, architecture, forms of entertainment, all the expressions of a people's identity are replaced. At first, while these changes are at the conscious level, there are protests and various forms of resistance. But in time, when the subdued nation "forgets" and the once-strange patterns move into the unconscious, the conquest seems complete, but is not really.

We are talking about how persons hear and why any hearing is in reality a rehearing. Experiences are layered; texts are layered. Preachers have always known this about the Bible. I am not thinking so much of those texts which quote prior texts or of those texts which quote prior texts which themselves contain quotations. Rather, I have in mind the countless times prior texts come to or near the surface of later texts in little noticed ways, as allusions and echoes. One can open a critical edition of a Greek New Testament and, even if one no longer reads Greek, the number of references to other biblical texts will be most striking. If one turns to those passages, in many cases the connection is but a word or phrase. Then one begins to wonder if the writer was conscious of all these sources and was working with research notes as a student does in a term paper, or are these imported terms, phrases, and images a part of the writer's compost. Although no single theory satisfies all cases, are we not in part observing writers being resourced by their unconscious memories? Luke or John or Paul might be surprised at how sprinkled with the Greek Old Testament their sentences are. I recall hearing years ago a preacher whose first career was as a college teacher of Shakespeare. His sermon was laced with fitting lines from a number of the plays but he never "quoted" Shakespeare. Since I was at the time an instructor in Shakespeare, I spoke commendingly to the preacher about it. He seemed surprised at my observation and confessed to being unaware of it. As I reflect on it, that unawareness on his part added to the effectiveness of the Shakespearean enrichment of his sermon.

Preachers who are readers of great literature have observed that, much like the Bible, these pieces, too, are layered and flavored with prior texts. I have used the words "layered" and "flavored" deliberately to mark the presence of prior voices and texts in a message in ways quite different from duplication or quotation. Exact quotations are valuable and sometimes necessary, as in legal matters, proofs, and settling disputes, but in communication such as preaching, quotations are vastly overrated. Most quotations are not easily portable; some value and meaning is lost crossing the border. All of us know from experience that sometimes the most irresponsible use of the Bible occurs in quoting a passage exactly. Often those who do it assume a triumphant air as though all is settled. Mind you, I resist at every turn misquotations and that cavalier nonuse of Scripture by those who assume that is the only option available to those wishing to avoid biblicism. All I wish to say here is that it is an error to think that quoting what Peter said in Jerusalem will be heard the same way if a preacher in Spokane quotes Peter exactly. Change the audience, the social and political climate, the religious heritage, the operative values, and even after a precise quotation Peter would rise and say, "But that is not what I said!" Well, it is, but it is not. In order for me to say in Tulsa what Peter said in Jerusalem I must say something different. As you know, Deuteronomy does not repeat Exodus; it remembers Exodus.

Not even during the Renaissance, when there was not only the rediscovery of the Greek and Latin classics but an adoring attachment to them, were young writers advised to duplicate or to quote the work of the ancients. Great works of art and literature have their best influence on us, not when we copy them, but when they generate in us something new. If, then, in the new creation one sees a subtle resemblance to a source, it deserves praise, not censure.

Thus in countless ways all that you read will enrich all your work. Such may have been advice given to the Gospel writer Luke: "Immerse yourself in the Hebrew Bible before you write a sentence." At least, that is the impression on the one who reads Luke from the beginning verse. The story is new, to be sure, but anyone familiar with the Old Testament feels completely at home. The Gospel is a twice-told tale.

But I see a hand in the air in the back of the room: All this sounds well and good for the preacher who reads, sees, and observes long and well. The reservoir out of which sermons flow is deep and wide. The streams that fill the reservoir and nourish the preaching cannot and need not be identified. Even the forgotten is not forgotten; it reappears as something new while giving depth and authenticity to the message. And all this sounds well and good for those listeners who have read, seen, and observed well enough to catch the references, the allusions, the echoes, and be stirred by them. But what if the hearers before us as we speak have no such memories, conscious or unconscious? What if my congregation not only does not know the Old Testament but does not know Luke, who assumes they do? Can I still preach from Luke? If so, how?

Those of you familiar with my work know that I have long held the position that preaching is not entirely a matter of "making deposits" (to borrow a phrase from Paulo Freire, *Pedagogy of the Oppressed*) of theological, biblical, and practical information in the minds and hearts of the listeners. It is that, of course; after all, there is a subject, there is content. We are not simply boiling water; we are trying to make soup. But preaching is also very much a matter of writing checks on what is already there in the minds and hearts of the congregation. Preaching effectively is calling out something from the hearers, letting them bring something to the sermon, offering their contribution to God as a part of that portion of worship we call the sermon. Good sermons are not only provocative but also evocative. As members of the people of God, the listeners both give and receive.

The most common criticism I have received over the years from preachers and homileticians is that my estimate of the listener, however well meaning, is completely erroneous. There is not enough, they tell me, in the memory bank of the average listener on which to draw a check of any size. All our biblical and theological references and allusions fall to the floor in front of the pulpit, unheard and unclaimed. And by memory they are not referring to recall, that rarest of all forms of recollection; they mean recognition. Recall is the capacity to call something up from the past and locate it in the present; recognition is the capacity to take something present and locate it in the past. Recognition is much easier. For example, I may not be able to recall the name of the city where the Liberty Bell is located, but show me a multichoice list including the name Philadelphia and I recognize it. Our sermon listeners, my correctors say, do not even recognize names, places, events, and theological themes that fill our messages from week to week. For these people, I am told, the sermon is not a twice-told tale, is not a memory.

Before I respond, I wish first to reaffirm the central idea that there is in the preaching and hearing of the gospel the experience of its being twice-told, that the hearing is in a real sense a rehearing. In some way not clear to me—call it human nature or the Holy Spirit—the gospel is a word for which we had waited and listened, and when we heard it, its affirmation and promise did not sound new or strange. Within the folds of its grace the soul felt that it had returned home.

Now, having said that, I acknowledge that my experience confirms the truth of my critics. There is an informational dimension to Christian preaching because the Christian faith is centered on incarnation, and, simply put, incarnation means God within history; that is, times, dates, places, events, relationships, real people with real names. These are not matters which are called up but which are looked up. We do not have access to this information by reason of our created natures or by the prevenient grace of the Holy Spirit. This must be taught, otherwise references and allusions to the historical content of the faith are lost on the hearers. For them there is none of Aristotle's "joy of recognition." As long as this is their condition, such listeners may drop out after a period of feeling like ignorant outsiders, or they may continue to attend but dismiss as unimportant "all that biblical and historical stuff," or they may request opportunities to learn. This last alternative is seldom taken, because a listener tends to think he or she is the only one in the congregation who does not know Joshua, Saul, Ruth, Mary Magdalene, and the sons of Zebedee. Given the woeful lack of knowledge of the biblical and subsequent traditions, for many of our listeners our sermons are, informationally speaking, once-told tales.

I mourn this lack, as do you, but I would be in deeper grief if, as an antidote, preaching be turned into explanations and definitions. Whenever and wherever that happens, the dove's wings are clipped and sermons crawl on the floor. To be sure, in all preaching one makes deposits of knowledge in the hearer's mind, but answering questions such as What is a Sadducee? Where is Gilgal? and, How do you spell Bathsheba? is not preaching. Preaching is the proclamation of the good news of God's grace, and information is appropriate if it resources and services that proclamation. The primary resource for such preaching is Scripture, but even a casual reader of Scripture knows that entering the Bible is to encounter, not definitions and explanations, but persons with genealogies, events with antecedents, relationships with histories, and texts that have subtexts. It is to walk into a community with a long memory, a community that has been believing and doubting, working and worshiping, repenting and praying, fighting and embracing for a very long time. The preacher knows that one cannot sneak into that community, steal a text for Sunday, and run. One must tarry and observe and listen. We are talking about preachers' enabling hearers to enter a community of faith that has been meeting since Abraham and Sarah, to listen to its stories and testimonies, to borrow its memories, and to appropriate them as their own. This is biblical preaching because this is what the Bible itself is and does.

I am persuaded that the congregation's memory bank, on which pulpit checks can be drawn again and again, can be significantly enlarged through regular Sunday preaching. The length of sermons need not be increased, nor does one have to bore the hearers with an opening segment on "background information." Eight minutes on Decapolis loses the whole sermon. But teaching does not have to be pedantic; names, places, events, and key themes can be delightfully and appropriately sprinkled through a sermon. Images, analogies, and easy-to-remember turns of phrasing can be vehicles for information received and enjoyed by listeners who have no sense of being in class. Often an appetite to know more is kindled, and a new door is opened. Girded by the principle of "need to know" in order to equip the audience with an ear to hear, such preaching never sounds like an admonition to "eat your biblical vegetables." Good teaching contains humor and playfulness. Seriousness of purpose does not require heaviness of manner. But, please; being light on one's feet does not mean being silly or bringing in the clowns. With most audiences, calling the apostles "guys" and John the Baptist a "weird dude" and Mary Magdalene a "groupie" trivializes them rather than bringing them into our world. If the anguish of King Saul or the tears of Hannah elicit from the preacher sympathy and understanding, the hearers will discover that yesterday's characters are already in our world. Slang is not needed.

But this kind of pulpit work just described is possible only for a preacher who is herself or himself fully at home within the Scriptures. And to feel at home there takes time: time spent in the texts, sometimes as a researcher, sometimes as a lover of good literature, sometimes as one on a faith journey, sometimes as a member of a very old and very broad community renewing friendships and visiting landmarks. Appetite for the Scriptures is created in the congregation by observing the awe and amazement, the silence and the shock, the humility and the transformation, the comfort and the joy generated in the life of one for whom living in these pages is both duty and delight. The preacher knows as well or better than others that in matters of geography, astronomy, geology, medicine, psychology, and sociology we have progressed light-years beyond those who lived in the centuries of the biblical story, but the preacher also knows such progress gives no license to mock, to ridicule, or to speak condescendingly of those whose burden and privilege it was to live at another time, in another place. A minister's obvious respect for biblical characters instructs listeners in the same, as well as respect for persons around us. Two thousand years is a long time, but there is a very short distance between an ancient and a modern whose labor lines the pockets of others, whose children leave home in anger, who wait for word from fields of war, who hold their first child, who wonder why God seems so far away, who weep at gravesides, who pray for the drought to break, who need the company of friends, who brag about amazing grandchildren, who are silenced by the surrounding presence of God. Listeners to sermons know whether the Scriptures are for the preacher fragments ripped from context to authorize a viewpoint or to serve as a hasty arsenal in controversy, or if they are the community's own treasury shared in abundance, with the clear implication that there is much more for those who are interested and who wish to return.

Having said that, let me repeat: even in those barren places where the funds of Christian memory are noticeably insufficient and preaching finds little information in the hearers on which to draw, still the sermon is heard as a memory. How so? The experience of the listeners, if not their knowledge, confirms the truth from the pulpit. Let me be clear: that which is preached is not the experience of the preacher or of the hearers. In other words, neither speaker nor listener is the source of the message. The source of Christian preaching is the Scripture, the normative record of God's revelation to us and in our behalf, but this revelatory material resonates with our experiences. How? Because we are all unusually spiritual and saintly? No, but rather because the biblical record is of very human relationships and events. "And the Word became flesh and lived among us" (John 1:14) expresses a truth not only about the Christ but also about the whole of God's revelation. One real problem of canonizing these writings as sacred Scripture is the tendency to remove them from the usual thoroughfares of human activity. We say, and we should say, that this Book is different from other books, but that difference, underscored by black leather, purple ribbon, unusual paper, and red letters, can move the Scriptures into isolated reverence. If we will listen to the history, the relationships, the biography, and the faith statements of this Book and then tell the congregation what we heard, their own experiences will confirm the truth being told. The preacher who relates biblical material and then says, "Now let us see how this applies to us," has created two different worlds, then and now, and must struggle to bridge the gulf. As I will attempt to say below, probing the heart of the text is probing the heart of the listener. It is when we remain on the surface of both text and hearer that differences between the two seem so nonnegotiable.

But there is a kind of preaching that stirs a deep sympathy with truth. Listeners to the truth thus expressed say with the lips or in the heart, "Yes, that is the truth. My life carries a thousand examples to confirm it, examples that lay so deeply buried I had forgotten their truth or their worth until I heard someone give them a voice." Such preaching is "lifelike"; it resonates with human experience.

For the communication event thus described to occur it is not necessary that we give voice to or draw on a pool of experience that is obvious in its commonality: that is, talk to urbanites about the inner city, to farmers about rural life, to veterans about the military, to youth about adolescence, to senior citizens about geriatrics, to women about women, to men about men. The value of that relevance is obvious, but perhaps too obvious. There is something about such direct and unavoidable connections that insults the listeners' breadth of interests and sympathies and their capacity for making connections. There are some experiences that have no gender or age or geography. For examples: dealing with a waiter who is cheerfully incompetent, or attempting to conceal an ugly scar, or photographing the three-candle reflection in a child's eyes, or canceling a doctor's appointment to sustain the illusion of good health, or feeling guilty about the dulling of grief and the fading of a crepe-laden promise never to love again. Such experiences join text, preacher, and congregation so inescapably that they volunteer themselves into our sermon.

But not even that is what I have in mind here. Rather, I am thinking of those actions, feelings, relationships, dilemmas, and decisions that mark the lives of persons distant from ourselves and our hearers in time, place, and circumstance but which nevertheless resonate with our own. To hear and see beneath and beyond the differences to the common human realities takes some work at paying attention, but think about it. How is it that Flannery O'Connor can sit on a porch in rural Georgia, write about uneducated southern Protestants, and move Roman Catholics in Chicago and vacationing Jews in the Catskills? Why does a Maya Angelou poem about poverty and abuse in Arkansas stir New York City to anger and compassion? The movie *E.T.* is about a green creature with three fingers and from another planet, and during the showing Americans young and old wept and cheered. Was there any pool of common experience on which to draw? Aged and crippled Vanna leaned on her cane at the site of old Delphi and spoke of times more ancient yet, when throngs came for the oracles seeking a certain word about the uncertain future. Her audience, twenty-four yuppie American students and their professor, sat immobilized, unable or unwilling to respond to the anxious horn of the waiting bus. Why? Where is the connection?

Of course, with the Bible we begin at a distance from the listeners, and we respect that distance. Collapsed too soon, the integrity of both Scripture and congregation can be violated. There are, to be sure, portions of Scripture from which all distance has been removed because all the historical particularities (Who? Where? When? What? Why?) have been jettisoned. Common experience, observed long and wide, has been distilled into proverbs and wise sayings, highly portable and totally oblivious to matters of time and place. "A lie will take you far but it will not take you home" receives a nod of agreement in any hemisphere. Gain from greed "takes the life of its possessors" is a truth that does not ask what century it is, much less what year or month or day.

However, with most biblical texts negotiating those distances is our responsibility, and we do so by listening to the text for resonances with the experiences of the hearers. Perhaps better stated, we listen for the truth in the text and express that in such a way as to stir deep sympathy with truth in those who attend to the sermon. You can almost hear the connections being made. What I urge, therefore, is the probing search for what is really going on in a relationship, an action, or an event. Most of us are not psychoanalysts, but we can think. When Jesus says, "[God] is kind to the ungrateful and the wicked" what is being said? The gracious and welcome sound of that sentence has within it contrary noises about justice, fairness, and the erosion of motivation for moral achievement. Until probing is done, the saying is not ready to yield to the symmetry of a well-framed sermon, a sermon that might be admired but which would stir in the hearers no deep sympathy with truth. When the battle-weary David longed for a drink of water from the old well back home in Bethlehem, loyal aides, at risk of life, slipped through enemy lines to grant their commander's wish. On receiving the water, David poured it on the ground. What is going on? Some real work needs to be done, because already the listeners are pondering: What ingratitude! But who could have drunk it? Would I have drunk it? Why?

We are, then, talking about laying bare the joy, the pain, the issues, the alternatives for living offered in a text, confident that such preaching resonates with the experiences of the hearers. And I hope it is clear that by resonance I do not mean simply agreement or identification; resonance also includes shock, resistance, penitence, and transformation. The preacher may anticipate but certainly not dictate the response. The message of a text is like a seed; it carries its own future in its bosom. What is of vital importance is that those who come to see God at work in the lives of persons not too unlike themselves will be open to the presence and power of God in and among them. We talk of three widows, Naomi, Orpah, and Ruth, huddled under dark veils, weeping and searching for a future, and something transforming is happening in the sanctuary. We tell of the witness of a woman of Samaria, and wonder how words so full of uncertainty ("He cannot be the Messiah, can he?") could be so effective, and a new boldness appears on once hesitant faces. King Saul, in the high noon of his faith, outlaws fortune-telling in Israel, but in the midnight of desperation puts on a disguise and visits the fortune-teller of Endor. One can almost hear worshipers long burdened by betrayal of their own standards saying, "There I go." Jesus talks of one-hour workers being paid the same as twelve-hour workers and the standoff between gratitude and resentment is almost palpable.

Whatever happens after such preaching only God knows, but one thing is clear: texts and hearers are engaged in an antiphon. Distances collapse as the listeners remember the truth.

Chapter Five

Not *What*, but *Who* Is the Matter with Preaching?

Marva J. Dawn

When the witty journalist and detective-story writer G. K. Chesterton was asked by the *London Times* "What's Wrong with the World?" he wrote in reply:

> Dear Sirs:
> I am.
>
> Sincerely yours,
> G. K. Chesterton[1]

Though other commentators supplied essays to answer the *Times* query, perhaps none could generate as much positive change as could Chesterton's stark reminder that each of us contributes in various ways to the world's evil and might, instead, be a stronger force for good if we were more attentive.

When asked "What's the matter with preaching today?" I immediately thought of Chesterton's arresting response. Instead of bemoaning the general state of sermons in the twenty-first century, I know that "I am" often the problem. There are many ways in which I could instead contribute more positively to the regeneration of preaching.

Of course, I'm not laying on my shoulders the blame for all the bad preaching of our times. I merely know, when my own preaching is less than the best, that I have gotten in the way of the compelling things God could do through me in each specific sermon and its context.

Just as I reached this point in writing the first draft of this essay, a call came from our clinic's mammography department. (It's been ten years

since I battled both cancer and the life-threatening effects of chemother-
apy.) Yesterday's X-rays might reveal a problem, the caller said; more tests
should be taken at a different clinic where the doctors can be handy to
investigate, though that can't take place for two more weeks.

Such an announcement puts this essay into sharp perspective: What
kind of sermon do I yearn to hear this coming Sunday? I certainly don't
want to have to endure anyone's trite opinions or shallow sentimentali-
ties. I long for a clear word of comfort and hope from the Spirit of Christ
Himself.[2] I thirst for Triune grace a'plenty.

Even more important, I'm scheduled to preach three times next week—
twice for college students and once for a parish nurses conference. What
sort of sermons will I give? How can I stay honest with myself and the listeners and still keep from letting my own worries prevent the Word of the
LORD from accomplishing its purposes?

I can't say what is wrong with preaching in general, but I know what
could be the matter with *my* preaching—and perhaps you recognize the
following impediments to effective preaching in yourself (or the clergypersons in your community for whom you pray). The greatest problems
with my preaching all arise if my "self" forgets its rightful place.

Don't think that I'm too critical of myself or that I have a poor self-
image or that I think the total involvement of my self in the preaching
process is not crucial. By saying that "I am" what's the matter with preaching today, I don't mean that we preachers don't embody the gospel. The
incarnation of the Word in our own lives is indeed crucial.[3]

Rather, I refer to all the ways that our own agendas usurp the place of
the gospel. These pages will sketch some of the ways that our sermons
might wind up with too much of ourselves and not enough of God, the
Giver of every good and perfect gift, the only Word that endures.

God *desires* to speak to our communities. The Spirit groans for us to
hear. Christ is still incarnate as the Word in our midst. This gives each
one of us tremendous hope and confidence for preaching: when "I am"
the problem, the true "I AM" is always at work in spite of me.

Pondering the Word

One of the first ways that I let my sermons degenerate is by not estab-
lishing enough time in daily life for God to speak to me. I think it marks
a weighty shift that the space for pastors in church buildings is no longer
called "a study," but has become "an office." That label moves clergy away

from the substantial business of devoting themselves to the Word and prayer (as in Acts 6) to myriads of technical details and "administrivia."

Of course, we can't help it. The mail comes; the people telephone; the committees meet; the business of the church must go on. It is a matter of priorities, isn't it? (Does it irk you to face that as much as it does me?) Do I believe that the most important thing I do is preach?

I confess: I know I don't always believe it.

I regularly need the sharp refocusing that the possibility of cancer brings. Next week I'll probably preach with greater zeal than ever, as if it were my last chance. But could I—every time I have the opportunity to preach—remember that "now is the acceptable time; . . . now is the day of salvation" (2 Cor 6:2)? What person sitting in the pews needs God's Word desperately today? Which ones are crying out for grace, a loving rebuke, forgiveness, truth, a reason to go on, a call to justice building, a reminder that God still reigns in the cosmos?

If I would constantly remember that the persons who hear my sermon all—each in their deepest selves—really need a word from the LORD, the great "I AM," then I would set aside all the time necessary for study so that I am as equipped as possible to give it to them. And I would let nothing (except for those same needs in their daily manifestations) interrupt my own listening.

God still speaks. Am I still enough to hear it?

One habit that has helped me maintain my study in the midst of office requirements is the practice of immersing myself in the sermon's text by memorizing it. If I learn a passage the week before preaching it, then my physical study gets expanded to the swimming pool and the airport lines, and my mental study continues in the workout and the waiting. God's Word invades my kitchen and bedroom, every chair and the shower. As a result, all sorts of new insights sprout, grow, bear fruit. (And many are rightfully allowed to wither.)

Often continued declaration of a text in my own mind reveals a structure for the sermon or makes more clear the chief value of a text in relation to the needs of the people (coupled with prayer for them as discussed below). Moreover, weekly memorization of texts (especially for those occasions when the congregation for which I'll preach follows the Revised Common Lectionary) deepens my awareness of the structure of biblical books, the significant literary traits of writers, the thematic developments of books, and the way certain images were "in the air" at certain times in biblical history. Fused with different insights gained by other aspects of my study, these perceptions give me a much wider grasp of ways in which these texts are relevant to the needs of the listeners and our world.

I can never know enough, but writing this section makes me hungry to let the Word of Christ dwell in me more richly (Col. 3:16), so that the Holy Spirit equips me more thoroughly to preach. The practices of study and meditation also provide more time for God's pruning work.

Pruned by the Text

Today I began memorizing parts of Isaiah 26, one of the texts for next week's sermons (and already chosen before the X-ray news). Another source of my sermons' shortcomings became apparent as I tried to retain the text: too often I try to preach to others before I have let a text prune me first.

Listen with me to this word from the LORD:

> The steadfast of mind Thou wilt keep in perfect peace,
>   Because he trusts in Thee.
> Trust in the LORD forever,
>   For in God the LORD *we have* an everlasting Rock.
>   Isa. 26:3–4 NASB

What a great text to chide me gently for my own fears and to rebuke our nation (right now when I write), as it ignores the world's pleas to refrain from aggression against Iraq!

The image of pruning comes, of course, from Jesus' words to His disciples that His Father, the vinegrower, pares every branch that bears fruit so that it will bear more fruit, and that they have already been cleansed by the word He has spoken to them (John 15:1–3). The text from Isaiah on which I am meditating this week in preparation for a future sermon keeps pruning away my fears by reminding me that God is trustworthy, a Rock on which I can base my confidence even when I am afraid.[4]

The text also makes it clear that in my sermon next week I will have to confess my distrust. Even more mortifying, Isaiah 26 reveals in this strophe one of the roots of my doubt:

> O LORD, you will ordain peace for us,
>   for indeed, all that we have done, you have done for us (v. 12).

I fear cancer because then I won't get all *my* work done. I know; that is really stupid!

Writing that makes it look so glaringly dumb. It is God's work anyway if any of my work will have desirable results. This text is a powerful pruner!

I used the word *mortifying* purposely in the previous paragraph because that is exactly what I don't want a text to be, and that is precisely what is the matter with my preaching. Unless I die to myself and my pride, I have nothing to give those who hear my sermons.

A prayer from the mountain people of Haiti makes this point well:

> Our Great Physician,
> Your Word is like alcohol.
> When poured on an infected wound,
> it burns and stings,
> but only then can it kill germs.
> If it doesn't burn, it doesn't do any good.[5]

If a text doesn't sting me first, I offer my listeners germ-laden words. I long instead to be willing to be pruned, so that I can join Timothy and "present [myself] to God as one approved by him, a worker who has no need to be ashamed, rightly explaining the word of truth" (2 Tim. 2:15).

Sometimes God's cleansing is a great relief. If, for example, I find myself lying awake at night wondering how I'll rearrange upcoming engagements if it turns out I have cancer, Isaiah offers me a way to turn that sleeplessness into a gift:

> My soul yearns for you in the night,
> my spirit within me earnestly seeks you.
>   Isa. 26:9

Will I remember that? Probably not well—but the more richly the Word dwells in me, the more it will prune away anxieties and prepare the way for better fruit in my own life as well as in sermons.

Again, Haiti's mountain people make this point well:

> Don't put your load of trouble in a basket on your head.
> Put it on Jesus' head.
> You won't have headaches.[6]

We wouldn't be human if we didn't have fears, doubts, anxieties, or other varieties of distresses, but the more we immerse ourselves in the promises and prunings and proddings of God's Word, the more those human concerns and anguishes can be transformed for our sake and the sake of our service to others.

But are we ready to read *all* of the Scriptures? A few years ago I looked back in an old Bible in which I had underlined many favorite passages. Not surprisingly, none of the texts that said things like "Woe to you, hypocrites" were marked. I've noticed the same in other people's Bibles too. And yet, "Woe to you, hypocrite" is a Word from God to which I should pay regular attention.

Similarly, sometimes we religious leaders discard texts that contradict our pet theories or ideological constructions. I need voices that question my prejudices and presumptions. I'm grateful that I can turn to faithful people who have written and passed on the Scriptures.[7] Will I let the "whole counsel of God" (RSV) have authority over me?

God still disciplines. Am I willing to receive it?

Formed by the Language of Scripture

Another reason that "I am" what's the matter with preaching is that I so often let my language be formed by the culture around me instead of by my Christian faith. George Lindbeck is the first one who taught me to understand Christianity as a practicing of the language of faith.[8]

Since I'm writing this while the United Nations debates a resolution concerning aggression against Iraq, and the United States keeps insisting that it will go to war whether or not the rest of the world supports it, I recognize the feebleness of language not formed by faith. I catch myself tossing around such idle phrases as "I hope we don't go to war" or "I hope somehow someone can change the President's mind." Those might be good wishes and fervent desires, but the only true *hope* for the earth is in God's deliverance from our sinful violence and failure to create justice for the world's poor. How much have I prayed *with love* for those in power with whom I disagree? I have sent faxes and made telephone calls, but do I think I can change the world with my efforts, rather than by the constant workings and interventions of God? Think of the great surprise of the fall of the Berlin Wall or of the Marcos regime in the Philippines. The question is not what I might do to change the world, but how might I be an agent of what *God* is doing? Do my sermons invite listeners to keep remembering that "indeed, all that we have done, [God has] done for us" (Isa. 26:12)?

Similarly, if it turns out that I have cancer again, I will certainly undertake whatever medical regimens are called for—but how often will I remember that it is God who does the healing, either temporarily by means of human science and skilled practitioners or permanently by taking me into the Triune presence? Do I let my faith and the testimony of the Scriptures and the faithful community form how I talk about illness and healing in my life and sermons?

Lindbeck asserts that it is not,

> as is often said in our day, that believers find their stories in the Bible, but rather that they make the story of the Bible their story. The cross is not to be viewed as a figurative representative of suffering nor the messianic kingdom as a symbol for hope in the future; rather, suffering should be cruciform, and hope for the future messianic.[9]

Am I letting the world redescribe the biblical texts, or are the biblical texts redescribing my personal world and the larger cosmos?

It is essential for my preaching that I view the world to which the listeners are in mission through the lens of the Scriptures. More important, regular immersion in the Word enables me to understand how God wants to work through me in that world. As Sister Joan Chittister describes the Benedictine Rule for daily Scripture reading, she questions us, "How can we hear the voice of God if we are not familiar with it? How can we recognize the ways of God if we have never seen them?"[10]

Various contemporary fads in "church growth" or renewal have let the culture around us describe the purpose of preaching. Then our work becomes the device of a charismatic personality to attract the crowds, or the means by which a church can increase its numbers, or the commodity that "meets people's felt needs," or the hyped entertainment that will keep people from hopping to another church.

Even if I try very hard to conceive the work of preaching in terms of forming the listeners to be the Church, the people of God in mission for the sake of the world, still the world's descriptions invade my work. I want my sermons to be "effective"; I want people to like them or to find them "uplifting" or "engaging." Those aren't biblical descriptions.

The question is whether the listeners encounter the Triune God in my sermons, so that the Spirit can accomplish divine and eternal purposes in them. How many of my sermons instead, when tested with God's fire, will prove to be straw (1 Cor. 3:10–15)?

"I am" the problem with my own preaching if I am not constantly being formed by God to speak and live God's language, so that those who hear will also become more like God. As a Haitian prayer entreats,

Lord,
We don't get mangos from
   an avocado tree
   and we don't get corn
   from the banana plant.
We produce what we are.
Help us to be
   what you need produced.[11]

Freed by the Holy Spirit

Our society so much values credentials, expertise, savvy, technique—but these can so easily be used to manipulate or to deceive. I fib to myself if I don't remember that I want people to like my sermons because I need them to like me. The question, instead, is whether my preaching will spur them more to love God and their neighbors. One of yesterday's readings in my prayer book reinforced this contrast:

> It is certain that a young man who fervently loves God, although adorned with limited gifts, will be more useful to the church of God with his meager talent and academic achievement than a vain and worldly fool with double doctor's degrees who is very clever but has not been taught by God. The work of the former is blessed and he is aided by the Holy Spirit. The latter has only a carnal knowledge, with which he can easily do more harm than good.[12]

"I am" the problem with preaching when I don't rely on the Holy Spirit to produce the results of my sermons—or when I quench the Spirit as I preach. For me, these two types of malpractice happen more easily if I write out a complete text for the sermon, because then I trust my own clever turns of phrase or my own carefully designed argument to convince the hearers.

I don't mean by those comments that we preachers ought not to be organized or that sermons should not be carefully planned and prepared. But I know that my preaching is more likely to be God-breathed if I immerse myself in the text, study like crazy, organize thoroughly, plan structures and progressions, pray assiduously, look intently into the eyes and souls of listeners—and then give the Spirit room to speak beyond my abilities. I can be so concerned about getting just the right word that I repress the Spirit's power.

Of course, the opposite is also one of my flaws. I can be so extremely impetuous that my spirit is not inhabited by the Holy One. That is why I need plenty of time to prepare a sermon—so that my spirit can be invaded, disarmed, and conquered by God's. I'm encouraged by the depth of the Haitians' simple dependence on the Spirit:

> The Holy Spirit is our boss.
> We know that he alone
>   remembers the route that Jesus walked.
> So we know that only he can
>   show us the same way.[13]

Willing to Risk the Prophetic Role

However, if I really depend on the Spirit, without a doubt I will be called to take prophetic risks. How can I authentically preach the Word which is "living and active, sharper than any two-edged sword, piercing until it divides soul from spirit, joints from marrow" if I don't let it do its work, to "judge the thoughts and intentions of the heart" (Heb. 4:12) of the listeners? But sometimes I am afraid—before or after I preach, or both—because I don't want to offend anyone.

An Ash Wednesday sermon in 2003 by Fr. Robert Rhodes offered a profound model of letting the Word bear the responsibility for its own prophetic work. The priest focused on Jesus' words, "But I say to you, Love your enemies and pray for those who persecute you" (Matt. 5:44). I have never heard a preacher be so tough as Fr. Rhodes was as he challenged listeners that if we are not fervently desiring and praying for the *shalom* of the Iraqis or the people in the parish with whom we disagree, then we are not really following Jesus. He dared us to weigh our hearts this Lent, to ask God to purify them and make us willing truly to love our enemies.

Several things empowered this usually gentle-voiced priest to speak so forcefully. First, he is an extraordinarily compassionate and personably caring man. None of us doubted as he rebuked us that he loves us.

Second, he spoke straight from the Scriptures. It was God's Word admonishing us and making a claim on us.

Third, he offered his own practice as a pattern for us. He told us that this Lent he would be studying two commandments each week and praying to grow in love for God and neighbors, and thereby seeking to become more deliberate in obeying God's mandates. He graciously invited us to do the same.

Inspired by Fr. Rhodes, I long to learn to be more caring in daily life, so that prophetic sermons obviously come from grace and not anger. I yearn to be more iconic so that listeners hear the Scriptures directly, without me getting in the way. I need to remember that a model can be offered, as long as it follows the apostle Paul's pattern, "Be imitators of me, as I am of Christ" (1 Cor. 11:1).

The Isaiah 26 text conveys several urgent calls for prophetic preaching. Consider, for example, this verse:

> In the path of your judgments,
> > O Lord, we wait for you;
> your name and your renown
> > are the soul's desire.
> > > > Isa. 26:8

I pray that God's grace will equip me gently to challenge the students to learn to wait, especially in times of international tension, for clearer insights into the Lord's ways and judgments. Some of the students present might be future government or religious leaders; will they be equipped by my sermon to seek constantly God's renown, rather than their own or that of any nation or church? Will my words deepen their desire to be formed into God's name (that is, character)?

Similarly, will I have the courage to raise boldly the issue of lordship by means of this portion of the text:

> "O Lord our God,
> > other lords besides you have ruled over us,
> > but we acknowledge your name alone"?
> > > > Isa. 26:13

What gods are ruling our nation now—fear, pride, our comfortable lifestyle, our inability to limit our consumption for the sake of sharing resources with the rest of the world? Can we, I must ask us all, claim that we acknowledge God's name alone?

Tensions are high in our nation right now; disagreements are strong. Can I learn to be loving enough to raise the questions gracefully so that the entire Christian community present can grapple more thoroughly with the issues of discipleship in these times?

Sometimes, rather than being afraid to risk speaking prophetically, I say too much. This Haitian prayer chides me:

Lord,
Help us not to talk too much
   because talking too much
   is like driving too fast.
Sometimes the brakes are not good,
   and we pass by the place where
   we intended to stop.
When we talk too much,
   we know we go beyond the truth.[14]

Prophetic words are no longer genuine oracles from God if I overstate them, issue them without the embodied truth of God's love, neglect to temper them with hope, or pass by the deep needs of the people who hear them. Again, I need to learn more truly to imitate Jesus.

Practicing the Prophetic Words Myself

It is an enlightening exercise to notice all the texts in the Scriptures that talk about being imitators. These passages invite us to copy the writer's fatherly anguish over fledgling Christians (1 Cor. 4:16), or the leader's giving up of any personal advantage for the sake of others' salvation (1 Cor. 10:32–11:1), or the believers' willingness to suffer persecution and still live joyfully (1 Thess. 1:6 and 2:14), or the faithful ones' diligence and patience as they wait for God's promises to be fulfilled (Heb. 6:12).

To be prophetic will always cost us. Am I willing to pay the price?

It might damage not only my reputation, but also possibilities for future speaking engagements or book contracts. It might cost me lost sleep or physical suffering. I might have to sacrifice the time it takes to talk things through with an opponent or to bear the stress of waiting for God's purposes to be fulfilled.

I run away from such pain. I don't like it these days when friends turn away if I try to challenge U.S. foreign policies. I took it personally when someone walked out of the sermon in which I questioned whether we could forgive a 9-11-01 hijacker if he had repented as the plane hit the tower.

How much am I willing to undergo to speak God's truths? Again, a Haitian prayer calls me to new attitudes:

Lord,
Thank you that You have
   given us the name Christian.
Now give us strength to carry it.[15]

Or perhaps I need this stronger rebuke:

> Sometimes we're no different
>   from the roach and the cricket.
> They pass by the Bible.
> They even eat at its pages,
>   but they don't practice its teachings.[16]

Am I willing to follow Jesus into the poverty of birth in a stable and later homelessness, the terror of being a refugee from Herod, the misunderstandings of His family and the incomprehension of His disciples? Will I accept the crowds' persistent aggressiveness and the relentless judgment of the religious establishment? Will I gladly bear prolonged fatigue or sustained discomfort for the sake of practicing biblical teachings?

God suffers for and with us still. Will I be submissive to whatever is necessary for the sake of obedience? How can I call others to follow Jesus if I am not eager to embrace the cost of discipleship?

Being Part of the Cosmos and Its Suffering

My unwillingness to bear suffering for the sake of God's purposes is amply demonstrated by my struggles with this text: "I am now rejoicing in my sufferings for your sake, and in my flesh I am completing what is lacking in Christ's afflictions for the sake of his body, that is, the church" (Col. 1:24). I am not exactly enthusiastic about perhaps bearing cancer again if that would serve God's purposes better—and yet I realize that my previous experience with it deepened my compassion for others similarly afflicted. I usually complain about my present visual, auditory, ambulatory, intestinal, nephrological, and neuropathological disabilities rather than celebrate that these too might be vehicles for God's power to be seen more clearly in my old clay pot (2 Cor. 4:7). And yet, ever since I heard from the X-ray center recently, I have been incessantly nudged by a yearning to be more receptive to whatever adversities could be useful for the work of God's kingdom.

(Don't worry: I don't believe God sends sufferings for such purposes. Our experiences of pain and deterioration are the results of this sin-sick, broken world and certainly not God's intentions. But I do believe—though it is hard to live the belief—that God can turn all these things into good for the sake of Christ's Body.[17])

The other reality that keeps insinuating itself into my brain these days is that to suffer cancer is nothing compared to the sufferings of the world.

I have been ashamed to realize that my adversities are nothing compared with the catastrophes that befall innocent victims of the world's wars and tyrannies. My afflictions are nothing compared with the tragedy of those 40,000 who die each day of hunger and malnutrition-related diseases. My burdens are so easy to bear compared with those millions, especially in Africa, who carry the grief of HIV/AIDS.

Could I ever develop the depth of devotion of the Haitian who prayed this:

> Father,
> They say that I am poor.
> Thank you, Father.
>
> May I also be poor in spirit,
>   that I may inherit the Kingdom of God.[18]

Could I learn to thank God for my poverties by knowing that in those places of weakness God abides? Could I let my own struggles deepen my heart for the world, so that my preaching always calls the listeners into mission for the sake of our neighbors? Could the immense needs of the world teach me the smallness of my troubles and the greatness of God's mercies? Could I, as a result of these three lessons, preach in such a way that congregants are mobilized by the Spirit's power for Christ's new life in them to fulfill the Father's will?

Being Part of the Body

Another reason that "I am" what's the matter with preaching is that I so often forget the gifts of the Christian community that support me. Sometimes I forget that the preaching task is not mine alone.

This flaw is aggravated by the fact that almost always I am a guest preacher and don't know very well the community for whom I speak. Yet they, too, have upheld me in prayer, and they sustain the actual task of my preaching with their welcome, their smiles and nods, their critiques and affirmations. Each one of us knows how much our listeners affect our preaching.

The Mennonites with whom I participated in worship and service during my doctoral studies were the ones who taught me that the Body of Christ can't hear all that the Spirit has to teach us unless we listen for the divine together, and unless all contribute to the attentiveness and contemplation.

It is like the process of writing this essay. My Haitian friend Elie Lafortune sent me the prayer book of his people, and their simple and simply profound prayers have affected how I think about this topic. The disciplines of the Benedictines, the wit of Chesterton, the testimonies of biblical writers—all sorts of Body gifts have contributed to this work. Moreover, I have shared with a few friends near and far my need for prayer as I wait to find out the results of more tests; these people have continued to pray for me, to call me and remind me of God's sustaining grace, to hope for and with me that the tests prove negative. Their fellowship has sustained me and empowered me to worry little and write instead.

Similarly, the Body of Christ always is part of how I learn texts, how I envision their connection with our lives of discipleship, how I discern what God wants to do with us. The better I get to know the community for which I preach, the more thoroughly they can preach through me for the glory of God and the strengthening of us all.

Why do I so often let my busyness or pride, my independence or fears, prevent me from receiving the Body's gifts for my preaching?

Being Prayerful with the People

Besides the reasons in the question above, I know I often fail to partake of the gifts of the community simply because I haven't spent enough time in prayer for the people, for the world, for God's wisdom. Some days I don't take enough time for my habit of praying the Scriptures, especially the Psalms, and yet this practice could be one of the best gifts for getting beyond my present anxieties for the sake of preaching. As Joan Chittister attests,

> Benedictine prayer . . . is not centered in the needs and wants and insights of the person who is praying. It is anchored in the needs and wants and insights of the entire universe. . . . Praying the Psalms and the Scriptures, I see with the eyes of Christ, celebrate God in creation, grapple with my own emotional immaturity as the Psalmist did, insert myself into the struggles of the whole people of God. Under this bright light of broadened human consciousness, I come to realize I am not the center of the universe.[19]

Sometimes I feel so guilty at my lack of prayer that I spend even less time in conversation/listening and intentional relationship with God. What a silly reaction! God is waiting to speak with me. Why am I so loath to listen?

Remembering God's Hope

Fundamentally, I guess I don't listen because I keep forgetting God's hope—the absolute, indisputable, everlasting surety that Christ will bring His kingdom to consummate fulfillment and fruition. The good work that God has begun in me, the Holy Spirit will bring to completion.

When I am filled with doubts and fears and struggles and hesitations to listen to God for the sake of the sermons that I shall give, I can confidently pray with the Haitians,

> Lord,
> There is a big devil called Discouragement.
> We ask you to send him away because
>   he is bothering us.[20]

Christ has defeated all such devils in the work of atonement, and the promise of our resurrection with Him enables us all to have confidence about preaching in spite of all the ways sketched above that "I am" the problem.

Therefore, I have immense hope about preaching for these reasons:

- Even though "I am" often the problem, God still calls me beloved and is always at work in and through me to accomplish divine purposes. God is always waiting to speak to me and to hear my call when I cry to Him.
- Even though I let other things clutter up my life, God still calls me to the preaching task and gives me new opportunities to be faithful in my study. And the Spirit is ever ready to guide my study.
- God still disciplines and works in my life to make me more ready to receive divine pruning.
- The Scriptures, by the Holy Spirit's inspiration, are ever available and trustworthy to form me to speak and live God's language, so that those who hear will also become more like God. The Scriptures carry the authority of the whole community of God's faithful throughout time and space.
- Though I get bound up in my own efforts and rely on my own skills, the Holy Spirit continues to prod and rebuke (sometimes through other members of the community of saints) to invite me to new freedom, the new life in Christ.
- When I don't have the courage to be suitably prophetic, the Triune God keeps giving me opportunities to speak the divine Word. The

more I look to Christ, the more the Spirit can form me in His gentleness and grace for the sake of offering prophetic words.

- Christ ever beckons me into greater willingness to pay the price of discipleship by the Spirit's power.
- When I get too caught up in my own struggles, God sends reminders of the greater needs of the world around me. Members of the global Christian community constantly call me to be more aware of the needs of the world.
- All of the preceding are possible because God speaks still through Christ's Body, the Church. Other members of the community will always call me to greater faithfulness for the sake of my preaching.

How can I not have hope?

In Sum

What's the matter with preaching today? I am.

What is right about preaching today? The great I AM.

I pray that this essay impels us all toward sermons that are less of ourselves and more of God. Then our preaching will be full of grace and peace and hope.

P.S. Now that this essay is revised and ready, I rejoice that further tests showed no cancer. But I'm grateful for the gifts of God its possibility drew forth.

Notes

1. Cited in Philip Yancey's "Appreciation," at the beginning of a republished version of G. K. Chesterton's *Orthodoxy* (Wheaton, Ill.: Harold Shaw, 1994), xii.
2. I capitalize pronouns used for Jesus (and other persons of the Trinity when such usage is necessary for literary flow) in order to emphasize that these are not ordinarily human, gendered words, but expressions of the divine mystery.
3. See the essay in this volume by the extraordinary preacher Barbara Brown Taylor.
4. See chapter 9 of Marva J. Dawn, *I'm Lonely Lord—How Long?: Meditations on the Psalms*, 2nd ed. (Grand Rapids: Eerdmans, 1998).
5. J. Turnbull, trans. and ed., *God Is No Stranger* (Rockford, Mich.: Baptist Haiti Mission, 2000), 96. The prayers were uttered by the mountain people whom she and her husband served.
6. Turnbull, *God Is No Stranger*, 86.
7. It is important to remember that biblical books were accepted into the canon because they were *already* acknowledged by the churches as authoritative. See John Howard Yoder, *Preface to Theology: Christology and Theological Method* (Grand Rapids: Brazos, 2002), 175–76.

8. George Lindbeck, *The Nature of Doctrine: Religion and Theology in a Postliberal Age* (Philadelphia: Westminster, 1984).

9. Ibid., 118.

10. Joan Chittister, O.S.B., *Wisdom Distilled from the Daily: Living the Rule of St. Benedict Today* (San Francisco: HarperSanFrancisco, 1990), 22.

11. Turnbull, *God Is No Stranger*, 2.

12. Philipp Jakob Spener (1635–1705), *Pia Desideria* (Philadelphia: Fortress, 1964), as quoted in *For All the Saints: A Prayer Book For and By the Church*, vol. 1. Year 1, Advent to the Day of Pentecost, comp. and ed. Frederick J. Schumacher with Dorothy A. Zelenko (Delhi, N.Y.: American Lutheran Publicity Bureau, 1994), 782.

13. Turnbull, *God Is No Stranger*, 38.

14. Ibid., 8.

15. Ibid., 6.

16. Ibid., 22.

17. My theology of God's strength and goodness in our weakness is elaborated in Marva J. Dawn, *Joy in Our Weakness: A Theology of Hope in Suffering from the Revelation*, rev. ed. (Grand Rapids: Eerdmans, 2002).

18. Turnbull, *God Is No Stranger*, 54.

19. Chittister, *Wisdom Distilled from the Daily*, 32–33.

20. Turnbull, *God Is No Stranger*, 36.

Chapter Six

Put Away Your Sword!
Taking the Torture out of the Sermon

Anna Carter Florence

Most of the time, my students give me plenty of reasons to rejoice in the state of preaching, rather than to lament its many flaws. Most of the time, they are a delight and an inspiration—as soon as the first few weeks of class are behind us, that is. Students who are learning to preach are, by definition, armed and dangerous; they instinctively approach the biblical text with swords drawn. The first order of business is to gently persuade them to disarm before they cut off any body parts. Happily, this has never been a difficult negotiation; my students genuinely want to learn, and basically trust their teachers. They have always agreed to put away their swords, just to see what happens. And as soon as they do, the text initiates a new relationship with them, the students fall in love, the swords disappear, and I can trade my hostage-negotiator hat for a piece of chalk.

I suppose this annual reenactment should make me wonder. If something really *is* the matter with preaching today, then sword-wielding seminarians probably have something to do with it.

Hacking Away at the Text

Let me be clear. The students at the seminary in which I teach are not excessively violent. I'm not even sure they know they *have* swords until the time comes to begin a sermon, when they instinctively reach for the sheath. Up to that point, they are as peace-loving and conciliatory a group as one could hope for. Not only that, they are biblically and exegetically *prepared*; thanks to the sequencing of our curriculum, they have been immersed in the ancient languages of the text, and they have all the shiny new tools for reading it. They can parse and scan, chart and contextualize. They can take a text apart and put it back together again in a decent exegesis paper. They can "live in the tension" of text/context, and debate the finer points of a postmodern or pre-Constantinian reading. By the spring term, when they land in the required introductory preaching course, even the most textually naive students have traded in their innocence for a certain level of interpretive freedom, which means that (1) the mourning period for Moses, erstwhile author of the Pentateuch, is over, and (2) it has finally dawned on the students that they can exercise some freedom with the biblical text without being struck by lightning. In short, they are a preaching teacher's dream: seasoned, still winsome, and ready to tackle sermon texts with the zeal of Fosdick himself.

I have tried to pinpoint the exact moment when the atmosphere changes, and as far as I can tell it is when we begin to work on our first sermon text. As long as the exegetical work is merely preliminary, the students feel free to delve deeply into the passage, assured that their questions and musings and rebuttals and conundrums—many of them insightful—are just a warm-up. But as soon as I ask them to move toward a sermon focus, all the shiny new tools and interpretive freedoms go into shut-down mode. The students simply freeze, like rabbits in headlights. It suddenly occurs to them that they aren't reading these texts for an exegesis paper; *they're reading these texts for preaching*, and they can't just wander around the text anymore—they have to get serious! It is almost as if tiny, invisible preacher people—all those who have shaped their ideas about what a "real preacher" and a "real sermon" are—set up camp right smack in the forefront of their minds, and start shrieking, "Enough playing around! You don't have time to 'live in the tension' when you have a sermon to write; you have to find out what this passage *means!* Your job is *to explain the text!*"

It is uncanny, actually. Those tiny voices can drown out everything one has learned about reading the Bible and incite mayhem. The students start hacking away at the text until they can grasp a piece of it to hold up, while announcing, "Let me tell you what this passage [insert any biblical pericope] *means*: it *means* that everything will be fine if we only have faith!"

Could this be a clue to what's the matter with preaching now? Why do my students think that the job of the exegete is to *explore* the text, but the job of the preacher is to *explain* the text? Why do they think that an exegete can lift up the tension in the text, but that the preacher has to resolve it—or worse, ignore it?

Sure, It's *Good*, but What Does It MEAN?

It would be comforting to think that perhaps the urge to explain is merely a phase, like adolescence, that we all endure; the swordplay, the urge to hack, all nothing more than surging hormones. Eventually (one could console the distraught seminarian) these powerful urges cease, and one *can* actually read a text for more than thirty seconds without wanting to dismember it. That would certainly be the preferable scenario. *More* troubling is the possibility that the urge to explain the text is not a phase at all, but an accurate description of the homiletic that drives preaching today—and this, I fear, is closer to the truth. Many of us, particularly (although not exclusively) in the Protestant mainline traditions, were raised to believe that *preachers explain the text*. It is what we were taught. It is what we *have* taught.

Justo González speaks to this reality in his book *Santa Biblia: The Bible Through Hispanic Eyes*, which contains a lively and wonderful description of what happened to him when he entered seminary and learned to read the Bible critically, with all the tools of the academy. González reports that he understood the texts much better, but didn't know what to *do* with them anymore; what's more, he didn't know how to preach except by imparting textual facts. This disorientation contrasted sharply, he finds, with the enthusiasm he had felt as a young person growing up in Cuba, when he believed passionately that *the Bible was good to him*.[1] Yet once he became a scholar of the text, seeking to understand it, González no longer knew how to let the Bible be good to him. And, like my students, it was the act of preaching that showed him this most starkly, because he was certain that preaching had to be about more than just explaining the text; preaching had to be about offering something *good*.

A difference between González's story and that of my students, I think, is that his particular Cuban context taught him that the Bible is not so much a source of guidance and information as it is a source of strength and inspiration.[2] For González, the Bible is good to us, and preaching offers that Bible. Many of my students, on the other hand, have been nurtured in quite different contexts. For them, the Bible is something sacred and mysterious that needs to be interpreted and rightly understood. Preaching is about *interpreting correctly*. Good preaching leads listeners to say, "The Bible finally makes sense to me!" rather than "The Bible is good to me!" Good preaching *explains*, so this thinking goes. Maybe that is what's wrong with preaching today—too much explanation.

This is one of the reasons we need poets. Poets are close kin to us preachers, I think, because they take words as seriously as we do: poets believe words can change a world. And apparently poets have the same classroom dramas that we do, according to Billy Collins, a poet laureate of the United States. Here is how Collins describes his students, in a poem called "Introduction to Poetry":

> I ask them to take a poem
> and hold it up to the light
> like a color slide
>
> or press an ear against its hive.
>
> I say drop a mouse into a poem
> and watch him probe his way out,
>
> or walk inside the poem's room
> and feel the walls for a light switch.
>
> I want them to waterski
> across the surface of a poem
> waving at the author's name on the shore.
>
> But all they want to do
> is tie the poem to a chair with rope
> and torture a confession out of it.
>
> They begin beating it with a hose
> to find out what it really means.[3]

If I didn't know better, I would swear Billy Collins wrote this poem sitting in the back of my classroom. My students are like his: somewhere along the way, they have picked up the idea that preaching is not about textual exploration or refraction, but about *solving the problem that is the text*. They cannot see it, hear it, feel it, or even wonder about it; they are too worried about solving it. And this stifles them. It keeps them anxious, fretful, and unable to engage in any creative conversation with the Word of God that does not immediately yield results.

Every teacher needs to vent once in a while, and Collins's poem offers a fine lament form to follow.

I ask my students to take a biblical text like Mark 1:4–6,
and hold the River Jordan to the light, like a color slide,
or press an ear against its hive
to hear John the Baptizer's ranting,
and the people moaning,
and the waters of the Jordan beneath a buzzing of locusts.

I say drop a teenager into the Song of Songs
and watch her probe her way out of her Britney Spears reality
into another world where her rounded thighs are like jewels,
and her belly is a heap of wheat encircled with lilies,
and she is beautiful and perfect in the body God gave her.

I say walk inside Jacob's tent the morning after he was married to Leah,
and feel around for a light switch
so you can pay attention to their eyes (*was* there surprise?)
as their retinas confirm
what their hands have already told them under the veil of night.

I want my students to water ski over the surface of Romans 8,
waving to the community of faith on shore, and calling,
"*Yippee!* Did you hear that?!
'*No condemnation for those who are in Christ Jesus!*'"

But these are puzzling requests, as far as my students are concerned. They will feel around for light switches and put on their water skis to humor me, but they don't see the point. "If we aren't supposed to be looking for what Romans 8 *means*," they press me, "then what *are* we supposed to be looking for?!"

Nothing, I tell them. Don't "look for" anything. *Just look.*

Tying the Preacher to a Chair

I am exaggerating a bit, of course: it is impossible to *just look* at a poem or a biblical text without *looking for* anything, because every reading has a context and a purpose; we read/interpret/preach *from* a particular place, *for* a particular group of listeners. But I have found the exaggeration to be necessary, because most of us preachers have forgotten how to *just look.* We are busy, and so sermon writing is a purposeful, result-driven activity with us. When we do sit down with the text (during the odd half hour we can squeeze in between meetings and the hospital), we are always looking for something: a sermon, preferably, or at least a sermon outline and a cogent sense of "what the passage is saying."

For Billy Collins, this is a recipe for disaster. Result-driven readings (of a poem, of a biblical text) are, in his opinion, thinly disguised "hunts for Meaning," which pit reader and text against one another, and turn the poem into a battlefield: "literary devices form a field of barbed wire," he writes, "that students must crawl under to get to 'what the poet was trying to say,' a regrettable phrase which implies that every poem is a failed act of communication."[4] Once the hunt begins, Collins warns, the reader inevitably ends up frustrated, because some texts (poetic, biblical) are opaque by definition; they do not easily yield a clear meaning. We don't automatically "get" them. And while the search for meaning is certainly *one* way to read a text, it is not the *only* way, nor should it ever be. Indeed, as his poem suggests, it can kill the spirit of the enterprise—which, for Collins, is fundamentally about engendering intimacy. *We read poems/texts in order to enter into relationship with them.* Explication and interpretation may help to move that relationship along, he says, but not if they are the only ways for us to experience the text, and definitely not if we move to them too quickly. Sometimes, we have to stop looking-for so that we can water-ski . . . feel for a light switch . . . *just look.*

There is another, more sinister side to the "hunt for Meaning," and Collins offers a wry and vivid description of it: students so dead set on finding out what a poem means that they will tie it to a chair with rope and torture a confession out of it. Our laughter at this hilarious image comes from the shock of recognition. Preachers, too, can take up rope and victimize a text. It makes no difference how humane or even unwitting the preacher is: *the "hunt for Meaning" is still a hunt, and all hunts end in violence.* Preachers who take on the role of explaining the text also take on the role of providing for their congregations; textually speaking, they may even be the sole provider. Every Sabbath, without fail, they have to come up with an answer that will feed a crowd for a week, even if (God forbid) the lectionary sticks them with Job. They do not have time, therefore, to dabble in leisure-pursuit verbs such as "explore," "question," "challenge," and "imagine." They have to be good providers. They have to *get that explanation*, and by any means necessary.

This is certainly a lurid spin to put on the proclamation of the Word (who wants to think of his or her preaching as a weekly hunt for fresh meaning?!), but there is worse to come. *If we preachers set ourselves up as the ones who explain the meaning of a text, then we slowly but surely kill our own relationship with the Word of God.* Intimacy is impossible when one party feels that the other is withholding things that are crucial to the relationship. We preachers cannot hope to nurture an intimate relationship with our sacred text in all its beauty and mystery, as long as our need to *solve* it overrides our desire to *listen* to it, and *look* at it. Problem-solving preachers have only two modes of relating to the text: (1) we can badger it and nag it to death, until it finally breaks down like an exasperated parent and raises our allowance; or (2) we can tie it to a chair and torture a confession out of it—a confession that may or may not bear any resemblance to the truth the text knows and really wants to tell us.

Here, then, is the awful outcome of the preacher's "hunt for Meaning," all the more sickening for its good intentions: when our authority as preachers rests in being the ones who explain Scripture, we are going to find ourselves resenting the biblical text and doing things to it we never dreamed we would do. And I don't believe *any* of us signed on as preachers because we sincerely wanted to crucify the Word of God.

Just When You Thought It Was Safe to Go Back into the Text . . .

My students would surely be horrified at the suggestion that their initial forays into preaching look more like the Spanish Inquisition than the proclamation of the Word of God. They aren't trying to torture the text! They are just trying to *preach* it, and somehow all the little preacher people camping out in the forefronts of their minds have convinced them that preaching is about having answers that make sense. So the first thing I have to do, as a teacher, is to politely open the door and invite all the tiny preacher people to leave class, so that our students can hear themselves think—rather like asking an overbearing tennis father to leave the tournament so his daughters can play their matches. I do that, and then I break it to them. I tell the students that their job is not to make the text understandable, or logical, or relevant, or fun. Their job is quite simple, really. It is to *preach the text*, because there isn't anything more interesting or sensible than that. Preach the text, offer it in all its thickness and inscrutability, and trust that it will speak better than we could to the competing worlds of consumerism and militarism and individualism and anxiety that plague our people. For a few months every spring, I am like a Nike commercial: "Just-preach-it-just-preach-it-just-preach-the-text!"

Except (and this is the understatement of the year) . . . *this may be simple, but it is not easy.* And not just because preaching-the-text requires us, as Walter Brueggemann puts it, to "speak truth to power," saying hard things that no one (including us) wants to hear.[5] No, I think the most difficult part about preaching-the-text is simply . . . *the text*. It is hard to hear and even harder to stand in. It is so thick, so baffling, so fractured, that "obscure" doesn't *begin* to cover it. We may think we have landed a promising sermon text with long-term potential—some fine, upstanding passage about God's love and justice—and more often than we would like that text will turn on us into something *so* unflattering: read on just a few verses, and God is depicted as absent, or silent, or just plain infuriating.[6] The text is brutally, unfailingly honest: God may be great and God may be good, but God does not always behave that way. God is not known for staying in character for the duration of the scene. God does not always act in the face of injustice; God does not always save. Unless we are actually comatose when we read, it is hard to miss. And how is a preacher supposed to explain *that*? How do we interpret conflicting reports (in the same text, mind you!) on the character of God that appear to counter each other, perhaps even by design?

There are at least two quite tempting options. The first is to *ignore* the text; the second is to *defend* it. Both are responses to the fear of not being able to explain. And when we are threatened by a text we find too difficult to live or understand, sometimes we preachers lash out. We attack whatever threatens our lives and faith, even if it is one of our sacred texts. Even if we have to hack that text to pieces in order to get hold of it.

It isn't deliberately sadistic. On the contrary—preachers ignore and defend all the time, and with the best of intentions: we don't want to create conflict. We also don't want to do more harm than good—which may be the result when a text is as confusing, conflicting, disturbing, and embarrassing as ours very often is. If we don't want our people to get burned or perhaps foolishly convicted by the Word of God, we may feel we have to *ignore* a particular text: take it out of the Common Lectionary, never refer to it, never preach it. If we don't want our sacred Scriptures to appear inconsistent or messy, we may feel we have to *defend* a particular text: sanitize it, domesticate it, drain the shock and stress out of it, even trump it if necessary, until what's left is "good news" (translation: "good news" for *us!*) in a manageable, rational form. For example: "This story in Acts 1–5, in which the early Christians shared all their possessions equally, is a romantic and idealistic view of economics that is not to be taken literally"—as if we listeners might go ballistic if the text were to offer an opinion about how we spend our money. Or: "The New Testament God of love has finally vindicated this harsh and demanding God of wrath we see in the Old Testament"—as if the incarnation were really a publicity campaign for a grumpy deity with bad press, and Jesus the new image of the kinder, gentler God.

I tell my students at the beginning of class that if they are serious about not ignoring or defending the text, there is one phrase they must eliminate from their repertoire: "Let me tell you what this text *means* for us." In my view, this is the quickest way to turn a sermon into a television sitcom. To take a perfectly good text and explain it, wrap it up, and make it smooth and relevant in twenty minutes or less, is *not* the preacher's job. No one puts a four-course gourmet meal in the blender. So there are some common refrains one is likely to hear in our introductory course. "Don't tell us what the text *means!*" is one; "Tell us what it *says to you!*" is another. How is this text summoning us into another world, the world of the One rendered in the text? Are there lumpy bits we can't chew, and bumpy spots we can't see around? Is it *so* obscure that we are seriously tempted to get out the laugh track and the blender? *Don't tell us what it means; tell us what it says to you!*—we preachers have to keep reminding one another, because no matter how experienced we are, it is hard work for us *not* to ignore or defend the text. It is hard work to say what we *see*, rather than what we *want to see*. It is hard work to drag our explanations backstage so that a simple view of the Word of God can have the spotlight. It is hard work to leave the lumps and bumps alone, and trust our people to do their own thinking, wrestling, and chewing when we could have made things so much easier for them to swallow.

The preacher's massive-yet-misguided urge to ignore/defend the text from would-be invaders has striking parallels with the story of the disciples at Jesus' betrayal in the Garden of Gethsemane (Matt. 26:47–56; Mark 14:43–50; Luke 22:47–53; John 18:2–11). Jesus' arrest takes his disciples completely by surprise: they are shocked, frightened, and clueless about how to react. They are also a little groggy from having dozed off (zoned out?) after supper, which must have been an arduous affair: *long* speeches (per John), distressing predictions, cryptic words about the Messiah having to suffer and die. Not an explanation or a caffeinated beverage in sight. They are (predictably) sleeping when the mob arrives, but it is hard to ignore armed aggressors; faced with a direct threat, the disciples reach for their swords, and one of them cuts off the ear of the high priest's slave. The bloodshed would surely have spread like wildfire had Jesus not sharply intervened. "Put your sword back into its place," he orders his disciples, "for all who take the sword will perish by the sword. Do you think that I cannot appeal to my Father, and he will at once send me more than twelve legions of angels? But how then would the scriptures be fulfilled, which say it must happen in this way?" (Matt. 26:52b–54).

A closer look at this story reveals some curious details. *Why an ear?* Why not cut off a hand, or slash a leg, or pierce a chest? In Greek, the word for "ear" is οὖς, and refers to sense perception as well as to cognitive and spiritual understanding: to cut off an ear is to damage a person's ability to hear words, as well as to take them to heart. But in this passage, ὠτίον, a rare diminutive form of οὖς, replaces the common word for ear; ὠτίον makes specific reference to the *outer* ear, and carries with it literary overtones of severed gladiator's ears.[7] This is a tantalizing buttress to Jesus' rebuke that "All who take the sword will perish by the sword." Could Matthew and the other Gospel writers (who also use ὠτίον in their versions of this story) be suggesting that the disciples, in their defensive mode, are no different from gladiators in combat, who mutilate their opponents for the entertainment of the empire? Are the Gospel writers making a burlesque out of the disciples' urge to protect Jesus by (of all things!) cutting off an *ear*—that is, the literal and metaphorical location for the human ability to hear and understand and *be saved*? Is the use of the word ὠτίον a scathing commentary of misguided intentions (cutting off someone's "ear" in order to "save" Jesus . . . ?!) that are hopelessly bungled, anyway (managing to cut off only the *outer* ear of a slave)?

One thing seems clear. Jesus has no need of disciples who defend him with the sword. In fact, sword-wielding disciples will not save Jesus' life at all; they will only lose their own. It is only a fraction of a step from here to the sermon: like Jesus, the Word of God has no need of preaching disciples who ignore or defend it with the sword of explanation. In fact, explanation-hunting preachers will not save anyone's relationship with the text. They will only lose their own—and with it, their very life in the Word of God.

"Can You Describe This?"

What, then, must we do? How is a preacher to manage, if she is trying to preach the text without ignoring or defending it? What *is* a preacher, if he is not the man with the answers? Perhaps we preachers are simply this: *the ones who will look, and the ones who can describe exactly what we see in our life in the text.*

Anna Akhmatova (1889–1966), the great Russian lyric poet, has a poem that speaks powerfully to this. Akhmatova was the most beloved poet of the Russian people in her lifetime. As a young woman in St. Petersburg, she moved in a sparkling literary circle, dazzling all who heard her recite her work; after the Revolution, when artists who did not support the new regime were increasingly persecuted, many in her circle left Russia for good. Yet Akhmatova did not. She understood herself to be rooted in history and the life of her people, and made the dangerous choice to remain in Russia and to keep writing. The government tried to silence her: her work was denounced and banned in the Soviet Union, her only son sent to prisons and labor camps for fourteen years. Akhmatova persisted. When it was too dangerous for her to write words on paper, loyal friends secretly memorized her poems for her—and so she continued to bear witness to the suffering of her people. In *Requiem*, one of her most famous works, she writes of standing for months in the Leningrad prison lines, during the Stalinist terror, and of a woman who "woke up from the stupor to which everyone had succumbed" when she realized the great poet was standing in line in front of her. The woman whispered to Akhmatova, "'Can you describe this?' / And I answered, 'Yes, I can.' / Then something that looked like a smile passed over what had once been her face."[8]

Preachers are witnesses.[9] We are artists, rooted in history and in the realm of God. When our texts and lives are threatened, we are the ones who choose (or perhaps are *sent*) to remain with our people, standing in line with them day after day, instead of leaving that text for an easier life.

Preaching is testifying. It involves an act of perceiving, and an act of describing. We preachers are people who have seen and heard something, and who have to tell about it. We are people who pay attention in the first place: we pay attention to sacred texts and human life, and then we try to describe what we see, even when it is beyond belief. Sometimes the truth we see and confess is so indescribable, so unbelievable, that we may have to find new words for it, or, as poet Anne Porter writes, "an altogether different language."[10] Our authority as preachers doesn't come from having answers or making sense. It doesn't come from being *right* about a text; it comes from being *true* to it. When our testimony speaks in our words and our bodies and our lives so that those who hear us believe that *we* believe, perhaps they will come to believe too. There is no other proof for what we say. A sermon is not something you can *prove*. It is something you have to *live*.

An Openness to the Emptiness of "I Don't Know"

Sometimes, testifying is saying, "I don't know." *I don't know* why God commanded Abraham to sacrifice his son Isaac; I look at the text, I see that it happened, but I don't know what it says to me and what I believe about it. *I don't know* why Rachel was barren for years and years, and I don't know why you cannot conceive a child, either. *I don't know* why Jesus had to suffer and die, and I don't know why your child is suffering while your friend's child is cured. *I don't know!* Sometimes, that is all there is to say, and we preachers and pastors know it. Sometimes, that is all there is to *see*, and we are the only ones who will look. But this is the holiest part of being a pastor, isn't it?—being-with, weeping-with, and *just looking at* what happens to us, such unbearable suffering and pain and joy, while confessing that we do not have answers for any of it . . . but *do* have faith in the deep logic and grace of God. Nothing in this life is certain except that we will spend a lot of time praying for explanations that for now are simply beyond us. "Our God," as Carlyle Marney remarked, "has a lot to give an account for."[11]

Preaching as testimony takes its life from the same spirit, but not many of us have been taught that a *preacher* can say, "I don't know!" Yet is the pulpit so different from the hospital bedside? Sometimes, the holiest part of being a preacher is being-with, weeping-with, and *just looking at* what happens to us, in our life and in our text, while confessing that we do not have answers for any of it—but we can describe it. We can describe what we see as well as what we cannot see: the deep logic and grace of God. And so we look, pay attention, water-ski, feel around for a light switch. We stand in the prison lines of an indescribable, unbelievable world that has somehow become *our* world; and when the woman standing in line behind us whispers, "Can you describe this?" we answer, "Yes, I can." *Yes, I can describe this indescribable place in which we live. Yes, I can describe that indescribable place for which we yearn. Yes, I can describe the hell we know and the heaven God promises; I am a preacher, and I can describe it, even as I confess that I will never be able to explain the distance between the two.*

All preachers sit in the "I don't know" saddle sooner or later—pragmatically, if not theologically. There are days (OK: weeks, months) when energy is low and inspiration nil; we sit down, look at the text for the sermon, and cannot see a blessed thing, no matter how we turn it. So we close up the books, go about the tasks of the day, come back again the next morning . . . still nothing. We may try to jolly the process along by looking up a few Greek words or flipping through a commentary, but the truth is that nothing is moving for us on that page; it is just dead letters. *The text is not intersecting our lives anywhere!* And then we begin to sweat in earnest, because how will we maintain our authority as preachers if we fail to solve the problem that is the text?

These dry spells are neither optional nor avoidable: they just *are*, and they come to each of us, with a vengeance, no matter how diligent or lax or eloquent we may be. "We have all been there, and it feels like the end of the world," says writer Anne Lamott; and that is true.[12] Yet few of us have been warned not to take it personally. Could it be (the Calvinist in us wonders) that we just aren't working hard enough? Could it be that we are not among the preaching elect? *Should* we be considering alternative careers? It is the preacher's version of writer's block, which according to Lamott is a misnomer anyway: "The word *block* suggests that you are constipated or stuck, when the truth is that you're empty."[13] The problem, she continues, is to *accept* the situation—that we are empty, like it or not, and that the emptiness is not a curse, but a necessity. Only when we are empty can we be filled again. Only when we admit that *we don't know* will we create space for God to fill. In fact, those three words are some of the most powerful and expansive that we will ever say, according to Polish poet Wislawa Szymborska. Szymborska was the 1996 recipient of the Nobel Prize for literature; in her acceptance speech, she spoke of how highly she values the words "I don't know":

> If Isaac Newton had never said to himself, "I don't know," the apples in his little orchard might have dropped to the earth like hailstones, and at best he would have stooped to pick them up and gobble them with gusto. Had my compatriot Marie Sklodowska-Curie never said to herself, "I don't know," she probably would have wound up teaching chemistry at some private high school for young ladies from good families, and ended her days performing that perfectly respectable job. But she kept on saying, "I don't know," and these words led her, not just once but twice, to Stockholm, where restless, questing spirits are occasionally rewarded with the Nobel Prize.[14]

Preaching as testimony allows for *absence*, both in oneself and in one's reading of the text. It is preaching that is not afraid to admit that *we preach the text, but only what we have seen and heard in the text—which is sometimes the emptiness of what we have not seen; at least, not yet.* I believe that such absence sets in motion a hunger that the Spirit moves to fill. When we have read Ezekiel 37 and are completely befuddled by those dry bones, when we have known what it is *not to know*, perhaps we are finally in a position to appreciate and even recognize the rain of the Spirit when it finally pours down on *our* dry bones. We can confess, "I had no idea for the longest time, but one day this is what I saw in the text; this is what I was shown. It is not the only thing to see or the only way to see it, but when the light finally broke for me, this is the part of the scene I witnessed." Such confessions help us accept ourselves as provisional interpreters, as people who do not have all the answers. They also model for our people a way of approaching Scripture: to read with humility and acceptance of our human limits and provisional wisdom—that now we see in a glass dimly, but someday we will see face to face.

The Preacher's Conversion: Choosing to Be Human

What is the matter with preaching now? That is an enormous question, a bottomless question. I used to think I had to be able to answer it. When I left the pastorate and became a teacher of preachers, I thought it was my responsibility to be able to explain to students, pastors, congregations, and colleagues exactly what was wrong with the state of preaching, and how to fix it. After all, wasn't that a homiletician's job, to be the pulpit's answer person? Wasn't that what the church and academy and tenure review committee expected? Wasn't a successful sermon a matter of the right form . . . the right language . . . the right image . . . the right theory . . . the right interpretation of the text?

What's the matter with preaching now? When my students started to punch holes in my neat lectures by preaching gorgeous sermons that broke every rule in the book and *still breathed*, I began to suspect that a "successful sermon" didn't hinge on mastering the right form or the right theology. Maybe I had been focusing on the wrong issues. "If your wife locks you out of the house," says Anne Lamott, "you don't have a problem with your door."[15] Maybe the problem with preaching had less to do with form than with relationships—*our* relationships. Our need to preach sermons that were right, rather than true. Our need to illuminate a text instead of living it.

I don't pray for answers anymore. I pray for preachers, that we will see and receive what my students embodied: that before we ever *preach* texts, we *live* them, and in human bodies. *We are not God.* We can never explain our texts, and it is not up to us to do so; God is the one who explains. Our call is to *be* in those texts, as the human *beings* (not "human explainings") God created us to be. Our call is to pay attention to the wisdom that comes from living in and living out the texts of life and faith, and then, if we are preachers, to try to say something about it. Whatever wisdom we see is only tentative and provisional, and that is as it should be: *human being* is a dynamic, unfinished state. What's more, it is so transparent that in a sermon, there is nowhere for the preacher to hide. I often wonder why we ever debate the issue of first-person stories in sermons, when we preachers don't need to say a *word* about ourselves for our listeners to know all about us. All they have to do is watch us "living in" the text.

It is a long wait until the day we will see face to face. Meanwhile, we live with passion according to the little we have seen and heard, and we preach this text and embody it as best we can, week after week, revising as we go. Or we could paraphrase Wislawa Szymborska, who said this about poets, but could have said it about preachers:

> Poets, if they're genuine, must also keep repeating, "I don't know." Each poem marks an effort to answer this statement; but as soon as the final period hits the page, the poet begins to hesitate, starts to realize that this particular answer was pure makeshift, absolutely inadequate. So poets keep on trying . . .[16]

. . . and preachers do too. Thanks be to God.

Notes

1. Justo González, *Santa Biblia: The Bible Through Hispanic Eyes* (Nashville: Abingdon, 1996), 21–27.
2. Ibid., 115–18.
3. Billy Collins, "Introduction to Poetry," in *Poetry 180: A Turning Back to Poetry* (New York: Random House, 2003), 3.
4. Ibid., xix.
5. See Walter Brueggemann, "The Preacher as Scribe," in *Inscribing the Text: Sermons and Prayers by Walter Brueggemann*, ed. Anna Carter Florence (Minneapolis: Fortress, 2004), for the development of this argument, and Brueggemann's striking proposal of "the preacher as scribe."
6. See Walter Brueggemann, *Theology of the Old Testament: Testimony, Dispute, Advocacy* (Minneapolis: Fortress, 1997), 317–19.
7. Walter Bauer, *A Greek-English Lexicon of the New Testament and Other Early Christian Literature*, 2nd ed., rev. and augmented by F. Wilbur Gingrich and Frederick W. Danker, trans. William F. Arndt and F. Wilbur Gingrich (Chicago: University of Chicago Press, 1979), 595 and 900.
8. Anna Akhmatova, "Instead of a Preface," from *Requiem*, in *The Complete Poems of Anna Akhmatova*, trans. Judith Hemschemeyer, ed. Roberta Reeder (Boston: Zephyr, 1992), 384.
9. As those who have read Thomas G. Long's *The Witness of Preaching* (Louisville, Ky.: Westminster/John Knox Press, 1989) will undoubtedly recognize, I am indebted to Long's image of "the preacher as witness." Yet I would like to push that image further and take it in some new directions. See *The Witness of Preaching*, as well as my dissertation, "Preaching as Testimony: Toward a Women's Preaching Tradition and New Homiletical Models" (Ph.D. diss., Princeton Theological Seminary, 2000).

10. Anne Porter, *An Altogether Different Language: Poems 1934–1994* (Cambridge, Mass.: Zoland Books, 1994), 30.

11. John Claypool, "Life Is a Gift," cites Marney in *A Chorus of Witnesses*, ed. Thomas G. Long and Cornelius Plantinga Jr. (Grand Rapids: Eerdmans, 1994), 125.

12. Anne Lamott, *Bird by Bird: Some Instructions on Writing and Life* (New York: Anchor, 1995), 177.

13. Ibid., 178.

14. Wislawa Szymborska, *Poems New and Collected 1957–1997* (New York: Harcourt, 1998), xvi.

15. Lamott, *Bird by Bird*, 178.

16. Szymborska, *Poems*, xvi.

Chapter Seven

God of Grace and Glory:
The Focus of Our Preaching

Mike Graves

L ook in your calendar and pick a Sunday, any upcoming Sunday. Then look in the Yellow Pages and pick a church—any church will do. Now imagine what you might encounter in one of those churches and the kind of sermon you might hear in that place.

On any given Sunday, the setting ranges from a rented storefront to stone and stained glass, the worship context from a brief homily before the Eucharist to a prolonged, climactic address near the end of the service, with an altar call to follow. Some preachers take to a solid oak pulpit, while others walk about freely "down front." The use of notes ranges from manuscript readers to extemporaneous speakers. The clothing ranges from liturgical vestments to business casual. Some ministers speak in natural tones of voice, as if they were discussing the merits of bran cereal, while others speak with such urgency the building might be on fire, or will be shortly. Some preachers look for funny material to fill the time and keep the folks interested; others parse Greek verbs, yes, Greek verbs, right from the pulpit. Some spin the biblical yarn much the way Garrison Keillor shares about a quiet week in Lake Wobegon; others move from "Point Two: The Power of God" to "Point Three: The Peace of God," always three points, always alliterated.

Of course, these issues only scratch the surface. There are more grave concerns regarding the state of preaching today than the architecture of the space, the kinds of clothes we preachers wear, the shape our sermons take, and the like. Namely, there is the content of our proclamation. When it comes to the substance of today's preaching, there are those who believe it their task to save the world, which in some cases means "one soul at a time," while for others the emphasis is an ecological one, really saving the *world*. Some preachers remind us about issues on the other side of the planet—genocide and rampant poverty. Others stress matters closer to home, the need for daily Bible study and prayer.

The content of the sermons preached on any given Sunday varies greatly, to be sure, which makes reading the preaching barometer all the more difficult, but the majority of preachers do hold certain constants in common. In particular, three claims make up the fabric of most sermons on most Sundays: (1) that a biblical passage/text be read and commented on in varying degrees; (2) that illustrative connections with this world be made, usually in the form of anecdotes or stories; and (3) that some focus or direction be given to the sermon, making more or less explicit the meaning of the message for the people in the pews.[1]

It is in one of these three claims that the problem with preaching today lies. Specifically, the matter has to do with the sermon's focus. It's not that the exegesis of texts is immune to problems. God alone knows all the wretched pronouncements uttered weekly under the guise of biblical inter-pretation and in the name of "The Bible says . . ." It's not that the hack-neyed use of illustrations worn thin over the years is immune either. Is there anyone who hasn't heard the "Footprints in the Sand" story fourteen times? In my opinion the more serious problem, however, is in the move toward what the text means for listeners, its focus. In the preparation of every sermon there comes a moment in which, with God's help, we decide what the sermon will be about. That moment, that move from an ancient text to the focus of the sermon for today—when we no longer look at the text through an exegetical microscope, but aim our telescopes into the larger theological solar system—that is where the problem occurs.

What's the matter with preaching today? In a word, theology is the matter! In so much of our preaching, we have lost sight of where to aim our telescopes, namely, heavenward, toward the primacy of God in our preaching. We settle for sermons focused almost exclusively on human behavior, and as a result the center of our solar system becomes us. In the move from text to sermon we all too frequently leave God out of the homiletical equation. Not altogether; no, of course not! All too frequently, however, we simply reduce God to the role of a demanding parent who, on yet another Sunday, requires something else from our listeners. We use God's name in our preaching, to be sure, but often in vain. We forget, grammatically speaking, that even if the *object* of our proclamation, what Fosdick referred to as the "main business," is to speak a relevant word to our listeners, God remains the *subject*.

In the move toward identifying the focus of our preaching (what the Bible means for the people of God in general, or what a specific text means for a given congregation in particular) we have repeatedly assumed that sermons are primarily lessons for how people ought to be living. This penchant seems stamped into the genetic code of preachers, ministers in need of a new kind of support group: "Hi, I'm Jim, and I'm addicted to moralizing sermons." And a roomful of preachers awkwardly respond, "Hi, Jim." In much the same way that Benjamin Franklin's aphorisms on hard work and good behavior became a part of American thinking, generations of challenging sermons have permeated our thinking about preaching.[2] In much the same way that teachers and students in public schools know that every Abe Lincoln story and every retelling of Washington and the cherry tree includes lessons on honesty, preachers have assumed every text, and therefore every sermon, contains a lesson on how we should live.

Even though the Latin word *sermon* means "a talk," and the Greek word from which we get the term *homily* means "to converse," somehow we come painfully close to the dictionary definition of a sermon as "an exhortation on morality" most Sundays. Many preachers, along with many more listeners, are no longer sure a sermon qualifies as a sermon if toes aren't stepped on, in Christian love, of course. Whatever happened to the good news of the gospel, that which God has done in Christ? As Robert Farrar Capon so aptly observes, "We've hidden the Gospel of grace under a bushel of moral judgments."[3] What is the matter with our preaching today? Theology. Theology is the matter (the problem) with our preaching because theology is no longer the matter (the substance) of our sermons, at least not in responsible ways!

This tendency toward moralizing at the expense of the gospel's good news has repeatedly taken the church down a dead-end road, theologically and homiletically. At the same time, we must not ignore Scripture's ethical demands. Dorothy Bass and Miroslav Volf, among others, have recently stressed the importance of "practicing" our faith and theology, and rightly so.[4] After all, the gospel is both good news and a call to discipleship.

A number of questions arise, then, with regard to the theological nature of preaching: How might we learn to read our Bibles differently? In what ways do our views of God affect our proclamation? What is the nature of the gospel? How might we clarify the differences between God as the *subject* of our preaching and helping listeners as the *object*? How ought we to think of our listeners in regard to a sermon's focus, or application? How ought we to think of ourselves as preachers? Ultimately, how might we conceive of preaching differently than as purely moral challenge?

"God of grace and God of glory . . ."[5]

My New Testament professor was fond of asking us seminarians, "If the gospel of God is the greatest love story ever told, why do so many preach it with a clenched fist?" Good question! If, in the words of Fosdick's well-known hymn, God is a "God of grace and God of glory," why does so much of our preaching sound anything but gracious and glorious? Every reputable systematic theology affirms that the essence of God is *love*. As Christopher Morse notes, "God is thus confessed not as being *like* love in certain respects and *unlike* love in other respects; God *is* love."[6]

Jesus repeatedly affirmed the love of God in his own teaching and preaching. In his first sermon at Nazareth, like a preacher returning to his home church from seminary, Jesus preached in the synagogue (Luke 4:16–30). As Luke tells it, the text came from Isaiah (58:6 and 61:1–2); and not surprisingly, Jesus' message was one of "good news to the poor . . . release to the captives and recovery of sight to the blind, to let the oppressed go free" (Luke 4:18). A closer reading of the Isaiah 61 passage, however, reveals a significant omission in Jesus' sermon: "the day of vengeance of our God" (Isa. 61:2). The gospel is *good news*!

This is where Christian preaching begins—with God's loving care for all creation. Why, then, do so few sermons start there? Perhaps more fundamental than the nature of the gospel is our understanding of the nature of God, which must be reexamined.

Frederica Mathewes-Green tells how her view of God changed when she converted to Eastern Orthodoxy. She vividly recalls when the icon of Jesus first arrived at their new church:

> From the first time I saw this Jesus' stern expression I felt awkward, as if facing someone who understood something about me that I did-n't, someone who understood why I have a murky bag of discon-nected guilt rambling about under the surface all the time. I know that I ping back and forth between this guilt, and oh-yeah? behaviors like overeating or showing off or gossiping or thinking luxuriously about how spiritual I am. . . . When I look into the eyes of this icon, I think he knows, and it makes him very serious.

Then she adds, "I had looked at this icon, somewhat shrinkingly, for sev-eral years before I realized that his right hand is held up *in blessing*. That is his will for me; he wants to bless me."[7] That is where preaching begins, with the love and blessing of God.

To emphasize God's love in isolation from God's reign, however, will not suffice. As the old saw puts it, there are ditches on both sides of the road. Jesus' synagogue sermon in Luke affirms that the gospel of God is indeed "good news to the poor," but it also affirms the demands placed on disciples to announce that good news and work for justice. Or, as the writer of 1 John puts it, the God who is characterized as love calls us to love one another (1 John 4).

"On thy people pour thy power . . ."

It was Karl Barth who exclaimed that God is not humanity said loudly. Barth stressed the radical difference and distance between God and humanity, a gap that only God could bridge. In his lectures on preaching Barth states, "All the action that takes place in preaching . . . is the action of the divine Subject. Revelation is a closed circuit in which God is both Subject and Object and the link between the two."[8]

Given Barth's thoroughgoing emphasis on God in preaching, one wonders what he might have thought of Fosdick's emphasis that the "main business," or *object*, of preaching was meeting people's needs, "the solving of some problem." Actually, it's not that hard to figure what Barth would have said: Wrong! At roughly the same time Fosdick was holding forth in Manhattan, Barth was busy practically removing humanity from the preaching equation altogether. God, declared Barth, is the subject, direct object, and even the verb! Nothing about listeners and their problems there! Commenting on this syntax of proclamation, however, David Cunningham offers a helpful corrective:

> The verb *to reveal* does indeed share the threefold structure of other transitive verbs (revealer, act of revealing, and that which is revealed: subject, verb, and object)—just as Barth describes it. But unlike many such verbs, it also requires a fourth element: the one *to whom* the revealer reveals (indirect object—dative case).

The grammar of preaching, notes Cunningham, is "incomplete without the active participation of those who *receive* revelation."[9] So the preached word comes from God to persons capable of hearing such a word, but for what purpose? Is God's message limited exclusively to ethical challenges (pleas, for example, to get involved in a soup kitchen ministry) and/or calls for repentance (warnings against lustful looks or too little Bible reading)?

The answers to these questions are rooted not only in the nature of God but in the nature of persons. As G. Lee Ramsey has noted, various anthropological models creep into our sermons and, like the bass notes of a well-known tune, often go unnoticed but have nonetheless a bone-rattling influence. Ramsey writes, "Informed not only by theology but also biology, psychology, sociology, and philosophy, preachers have an implicit understanding of the human being that draws from various sources. When it comes time to preach, we don't usually ask ourselves, Now what am I saying about human nature in this sermon?"[10] No doubt, more preachers should!

Thomas Long tells the story of a veteran minister who during three decades of ordination exams was fond of asking the same question. At some point in the meeting he would ask the candidate to look out the window and describe passersby in theological terms. The response usually took one of two forms: "Whether he or she knows it or not, that person is a child of God, loved and upheld by the grace of God in Jesus Christ," or "That person is a sinner in need of the redemption of Jesus Christ." Both answers are right, of course, but in this minister's experience those who stressed the love of God made the better ministers.[11] Both views are indeed right, but the Bible's *first* story involving humanity testifies that human beings are made in God's image (Gen. 1). Images of sin and disobedience are in the third chapter of Genesis, not the first—but somehow preachers get that backward at times.

There is an even bigger anthropological problem, though. Just as God both loves us and calls us to discipleship at the same time, humanity is more than persons who sometimes sin, although you wouldn't know it by the preaching one hears these days. Marcus Borg identifies three "macrostories" from the Old Testament, each with implications for reading the Bible: the exodus story that portrays Israel's bondage in Egypt, the exile story that recounts Israel's despair, and the priestly story that deals with sin and forgiveness.[12] Borg notes that all three stories gave shape to Judaism and eventually the ministry of Jesus, but that the church's preachers latched onto the priestly story almost exclusively, even though the other two were more formative and "primal."

Why, therefore, does so much preaching neglect people's despair and bondage in favor of harping on sin, things done (bursts of temper and the like) and things undone (issues of justice ignored)? Frederick Buechner tells the story of one Easter morning's service in which the preacher, "a good and intelligent man, looked out at his congregation toward the start of his sermon and asked if there were any of us there who weren't ashamed of our lives. I wanted to hurl him bodily out of the pulpit and put Borg there instead."[13] What he wanted Marcus Borg to share was how the story of humanity's sin is not the only narrative that defines who we are as Christians. In other words, our preaching should not only proclaim forgiveness for sins but freedom from bondage and some measure of solace for the despairing. The nature of humanity demands a more holistic approach to preaching than pulpit pounding.

"Crown thine ancient church's story . . ."

The first witness of Scripture, the "ancient church's story," is of what God has done, not what we are called to do. Old Testament scholar James Sanders notes how the Torah "is first and foremost a story about the mighty acts of God in creating a covenant people."[14] Rabbinic tradition views law as God's gift to Israel, not burdensome rules. In fact, some scholars are even willing to translate the Decalogue in the indicative: "Because you are my people, you *will* have no other gods before me."[15] The same can be said for the witness of the New Testament, which "isn't about guilt at all," notes Robert Farrar Capon, "it's about forgiveness. The Lamb of God has *taken away* the sins of the world, not laid them on us like a coat of tar."[16]

Consider, for example, the grand narrative of God's doings woven into the rhythms of the Christian year and its lectionary readings. The three-year cycle of readings is nothing if not primarily the story of God's mighty acts, of Israel's release from Egyptian bondage and Jesus' resurrection from the dead (both primal stories in their respective testaments). That is the story we rehearse over a lifetime of Sundays.

In Year A, for instance, the Advent season stresses the gift of God come in Christ to "save his people from their sins"(Matt. 1:18–25), as well as the coming "peaceable kingdom" when "the wolf shall live with the lamb" (Isa. 11:1–10), a reign that God will initiate. At Christmas, the first chapter of John's Gospel speaks poetically of the preexistent Word who became flesh and pitched his tent among us (John 1:1–14). In Christmastide we read how the Christ child is protected from Herod's schemes, a protection that Matthew hoped would be extended to his church, just as we hope the same for ours (Matt. 2:13–23).

In Epiphany we listen to Jesus speak words of comfort: "Blessed are the poor in spirit, for theirs is the kingdom of heaven. Blessed are those who mourn, for they will be comforted . . ." (Matt. 5:1–12). He does not challenge those present to become poor in spirit or to take up a posture of mourning, but pronounces a blessedness on those who already are destitute and grieving.

In Lent as believers relive Jesus' journey to Jerusalem, we are reminded of the journeys of Abram, whom God promised to bless (Gen. 12:1–4). We also hear promises of resurrection, both in Israel's life (Ezek. 37:1–14) and that of Lazarus (John 11:1–45). The redemption that will be accomplished on the cross is clearly God's doing.

Christ's passion as a suffering servant (Isa. 50:4–9) and his resurrection from the dead (Matt. 28:1–10) testify to God's faithfulness. Darkness gives way to Easter dawn and the good news that "he has been raised." Passive voice. This is God's doing! In the weeks that follow we read of a Christ made known "in the breaking of the bread" (Luke 24:13–35), who even as he ascends, promises the coming of the Spirit (Luke 24:44–53). And the Spirit does come at Pentecost (Acts 2:1–21)!

On the Sunday after Pentecost we read of disciples who are sent forth to bear good news for all peoples (Matt. 28:16–20), which, thanks be to God, eventually included us. And finally, in the long stretch of Ordinary Time we encounter a Christ who calls even tax collectors to follow him (Matt. 9:9–13) and who is with his followers amidst starvation (Matt. 14:13–21) and storms (Matt. 14:22–33). The central plot of the Bible's grand narrative is *good news,* because God is faithful!

But just as it is the nature of God both to be loving and to exercise dominion, and it is the nature of humanity to be more than sinners, it is also the nature of the gospel to be more than just good news. On the same Advent Sunday that we hear of God's peaceable kingdom, we are encouraged to "welcome one another" (Rom. 15:4–13). The Christ who speaks words of blessedness in Epiphany also warns against coming to the altar without first being reconciled to our brothers and sisters (Matt. 5:21–37). The Lenten journey that will include promises of resurrection begins on Ash Wednesday with confession of sin (Ps. 51:1–17).

The One who breaks bread on the night of his betrayal also calls us to love one another (John 13:31–35). The Christ who is with his disciples amidst starvation also calls us to feed the hungry and visit those in prison (Matt. 25:31–46).

What, then, of the Bible's ethical demands? What are preachers to do with the challenges of Holy Scripture? For instance, what about the call in both testaments to be holy even as God is holy (Lev. 11:44–45; 1 Pet. 1:15–16), or to love God and neighbor (Deut. 6:5; Lev. 19:18; Matt. 22:34–40)? What of recent emphases on "practicing" the disciplines of our faith?

In Wayne Meeks's classic work, *The Origins of Christian Morality*, he notes: "When the early Christians talked about human behavior, they also talked about God, usually in the same breath." He adds that one of the chief characteristics of Christian ethics, which was inherited from Judaism, is the notion that God "wants a people to behave in a certain way and takes measures to enable and encourage them to do so."[17]

Meeks points to both the epistles of Paul and the Gospels as examples of the moral demands the Scriptures make. From the "letter of moral advice" called 1 Thessalonians (the earliest Christian document) to the sayings of Jesus, which often "exemplify the moral attitudes a follower of Jesus ought to have," the writings of the New Testament "are concerned with the way converts to the movement ought to behave."[18]

Properly understood, then, gospel preaching need not choose between what God has done in Christ and how we are to respond as Christ's followers. Victor Paul Furnish is helpful when he notes the interrelatedness of the apostle Paul's indicatives and imperatives, how they stand "in the closest connection" with each other. Furnish stresses that obedience to God is not a prerequisite to new life in Christ, nor a result of it either. "Obedience is *constitutive* of the new life."[19] Granted, this interrelatedness is not easily comprehended. Perhaps it helps to recall that the "fruit of the Spirit," that which the Spirit produces in our lives, ends with "self-control," that which we are exhorted to produce in God (Gal. 5:22–23).

Lest we oversimplify matters, this interrelatedness is evident in the Bible's narrative literature too.[20] In both testaments, the stories of our faith invite us to respond, not just listen. James McClendon notes that the Gospels, for instance, invite us to identify with the characters we encounter there. "This story," he writes, "becomes moral demand, moral guidance, moral *telos* for readers just to the extent that we get the point of the story, recognize the one there called Christ as our Lord, and thus confess ourselves to be among the disciples in the kingdom."[21]

"Bring its bud to glorious flower . . ."

Every Sunday we preachers dare to say something about God and gospel, to move ever closer in bringing the church's "bud to glorious flower," or at least so we hope. How, then, shall we preach? Is it possible to aim our telescopes heavenward without losing sight of the church's humanity? How do we honor the dialectical tensions related to the nature of God? the nature of humanity? the nature of the gospel? How might preaching be viewed as something other than a harangue in the name of an angry, or at least demanding, God? Whatever happened to the good news of the gospel?

As the evidence shows, anecdotal and otherwise, the preaching of good news has come on hard times. Consider, for example, some of the harsh sermons by preachers in literature. In *Huckleberry Finn*, Mark Twain portrays a minister railing against sin at a Parkville camp meeting. In *Tobacco Road*, Erskine Caldwell's character, Sister Bessie, goes so far as to describe the essence of preaching as being "*against* something":

> Preachers has got to preach *against* something. It wouldn't do them no good to preach *for* everything. They got to be *against* something every time. . . . Good preachers don't preach about God and heaven, and things like that. They always preach *against* something, like hell and the devil. Them is things to be against. It wouldn't do a preacher no good to preach for God. He's got to preach against the devil and all wicked and sinful things. That's what the people like to hear about. They want to hear about the bad things.[22]

More recently, Barbara Kingsolver's haunting portrayal of the Baptist preacher Nathan Price in *The Poisonwood Bible* ought to send chills down the backs of preachers everywhere. Along with his wife and four daughters, the Reverend Price (always "Father" to his family members) lands in the Congo to evangelize the heathen. Asked to say a blessing over a meal, his first act of ministry in a new setting, he instead rants against the bare-breasted women of the tribe. One of his young daughters describes the scene: "He was getting that look he gets, oh boy, like Here comes Moses tromping down off of Mount Syanide with ten fresh ways to wreck your life."[23]

In *The Seven Storey Mountain*, Thomas Merton describes a school chaplain whose own preaching and teaching resulted in "an obscure mixture of ideals of English gentlemanliness and his favorite notions of personal hygiene." Commenting on the chaplain's exegesis of 1 Corinthians 13, Merton writes that, in essence, the fellow simply substituted "gentleman" for "charity" throughout the chapter: "A gentleman is patient, is kind; a gentleman envieth not, dealeth not perversely, is not puffed up. . . . A gentleman never falleth away." Merton then adds, "I think St. Peter and the twelve Apostles would have been rather surprised at the concept that Christ had been scourged and beaten by soldiers, cursed and crowned with thorns and subjected to unutterable contempt and finally nailed to the Cross and left to bleed to death in order that we might all become gentlemen."[24]

Unfortunately, the evidence for rampant moralizing these days is more than anecdotal. Marsha Witten's sociological study of sermons by Southern Baptists and preachers of the Presbyterian Church (U.S.A.) reveals appalling trends. Limiting her study to messages based on the parable of the prodigal son, she found that most were guilt-producing, with roughly only one-fourth of the sermons emphasizing God's extravagant love toward humanity.[25] In other words, instead of describing the party to which all of God's children—both wayward and faithful—are invited, listeners are scolded for not coming.

If Harry Emerson Fosdick is right that one of the measures of a sermon's effectiveness is how many people wish to see the minister alone after the sermon, it is no wonder that most Sundays the people simply file through the line, repeating banalities such as, "Good sermon, preacher." "Enjoyed the service." "You really hit the nail on the head this morning, preacher." Banalities, sure, but private conversation? No, thanks. Who, in their right mind, would want to have a cup of coffee with a rabid prophet? I know parents who tell me that their kids are actually scared of their minister. "Why is the preacher always so mad, Mommy?" Somehow Paul's statement about preaching Christ crucified (1 Cor. 1:23) becomes in the mouths of some preachers a license to crucify the listeners.

But not always and not everywhere. The very same literature (and movies) that often portray preachers raging wildly against sin, on other occasions depict benign ministers, usually caricatures of Roman Catholic priests, who are willing to grant absolution haphazardly or to offer an insipid homily of no real consequence. In real life, sometimes it comes from a crystal-throated preacher in a church of glass (where I suppose ministers aren't supposed to throw stones), at other times from the liberal, mainline church where parishioners, we are told, do not care much for judgment themes, thank you very much. Even so-called justice preaching often degenerates into moralizing, only on a grander scale. What, the preacher asks, are we going to do about world hunger? The gospel's flower buds fullest, however, when we are faithful to both its good news and its demands of discipleship. How, then, shall we preach?

"Grant us wisdom, grant us courage . . ."

In Herman Stuempfle's classic study, *Preaching Law and Gospel*, he wonders why preachers find it easier to harp on the negative than to share the gospel's good news:

> Is it because in a fallen world images of sin and brokenness always
> seem closer at hand than images of grace? Is it because we as preach-
> ers find some strange corner of our egos more satisfied by exposing

darkness than by announcing light? Is it because we ourselves scarcely believe the astonishing news of our own liberation, and therefore feel too little compulsion to speak it to others?[26]

Whatever the reasons, Stuempfle is surely correct when he notes that at least part of the problem is a misreading of the church's Scripture, wherein we discover that the Bible's "single plot" is grace.[27] Unfortunately, even in our childhood moralizing tendencies are driven home, when stories of generous Abraham are turned into Aesop's Fables for the faithful: "Children, God wants us to be like Abraham." Never mind that in the next few chapters of Genesis Abraham will lie and give his wife over to a stranger. Not once, but twice! We forget that the Bible, especially the Bible's narratives, are mirrors before they are morals. We read the stories of Scripture with such delight because we see ourselves in them, people who are sometimes generous, sometimes not, but whom God always treats with love and justice even as we are called to enter into covenant with God.

When we limit our reading of Scripture to themes of sin, judgment, and forgiveness alone, we forget that the Bible is more than a "hammer of judgment," to use Martin Luther's term, but also what Paul Tillich labeled a "mirror of existence."[28] Commenting on the relevance of the latter for contemporary preaching, Stuempfle describes the gospel as an "antiphon to existence," with one of the goals of preaching being to describe a different way of being in the world.[29] The gospel as antiphon—a different sound. Description, not accusation, becomes the focus of such preaching, reading the Scriptures as what James Sanders describes as the *constitutive* narrative of God's people (that which *constitutes*, or makes up, who we are).[30]

This constitutive reading places the stress on what God has done to form a covenant people. Theocentric reading strategies call us as preachers to identify in biblical texts the action God has taken and is taking on our behalf, and to do so *before* we ever consider any lesson related to our own behavior. Unfortunately, we often get that backward. Somehow the valley of dry bones that God brings back to life (Ezek. 37) becomes the valley where if we try hard enough and make ourselves available to God, we can rise up and do great things. That's not gospel! Somehow the mount where Abraham discovers firsthand that "the LORD will provide" (Gen. 22) becomes the mount where the old patriarch gave it his all, and if we do the same, we will be able to do great things as well. Such so-called preaching sounds more like the self-help section at Barnes & Noble than gospel.[31]

How, then, shall we preach? G. Lee Ramsey stresses the need for indicative portrayals of what God hopes for the church. Listeners need to be told not just to care, for instance, but to see what a caring church looks like. Instead of chastising the congregation for not doing enough to feed the poor, the minister might commend them for what they are already doing, for if the truth be told, most congregations already sustain many social justice programs, even if they could do more. As Ramsey describes it, the preacher "holds the mirror up to the congregation and says, 'See who we are,' while at the same time reminding them of how they have become who they are through the provision of God."[32]

In my own preaching I have found that such indicative preaching not only reminds us who we are as the people of God, but in subtle ways challenges us to live up to that identity. To make my point, I occasionally tell my students: "Imagine if I came to class one morning and bragged on one of you. 'Nikki, your sermon was absolutely brilliant the other day. You do really fine work!'" On the one hand, Nikki has received a compliment, in the indicative voice. On the other hand, she has been issued a challenge, still in the indicative voice but with an implied imperative. Maybe our grandparents were right—the carrot is better than the stick.

Theocentric reading strategies, then, involve paying attention to our grammar (indicative versus imperative), as well as the constitutive nature of Scripture (descriptive versus prescriptive). But a theocentric focus need not ignore the prophetic nature of Scripture. Even Fosdick's emphasis on sermons' meeting people's needs includes both comfort and challenge—not just puzzling personal problems, but also "a sin that has come perilously close to wrecking them."

When the moment comes to decide what the sermon will be about, prophetic *and* constitutive possibilities are present, perhaps both in the same sermon. With most any passage of Scripture we can find challenging and comforting options. Therefore, we ministers ought to pray for wisdom, to know what word is needed for the moment.

Take, for instance, a Gospel reading from the Third Sunday in Lent of Year A—the story of Jesus and the Samaritan woman (John 4:5–42). Our first tendency, as we have seen, is to assume a lesson is present, some challenge for our listeners. No doubt such a reading is possible. There is, for example, the possibility of identifying with the disciples who are shocked that Jesus would speak with such an outcast. The sermon could challenge our own tendency to erect barriers, all in the name of orthodoxy, of course. A responsible reading would emphasize that such a challenge emanates first out of the nature of God's Christ, who accepts all persons. Such a reading will most definitely preach.

There is another possibility, however—one that not only begins with a theocentric (or in this case, Christocentric) focus but stays there, resulting in a constitutive reading. Most of us who have preached from this story recall how the woman had "three strikes" against her: a Samaritan in a Jewish world; a woman in a man's world, and five husbands. For whatever reasons, we generally assume the last strike is a moral judgment against her. Never mind the fact that in the ancient Mediterranean world to have had five husbands probably means she was repeatedly abandoned, left without financial means.

Some who have preached from this story may also recall the literary form that the text brings to mind, namely, Old Testament courtship rituals. More than once, Genesis tells stories of courtship that began at a well. The story in John's Gospel tells of Jesus' coming to this nameless woman in an offer of courtship. She who had been shunned by society and her community (she draws water at the unlikely time of noon) is accepted by the Christ. Such a reading is gospel, good news! Those who have been rejected are accepted by God!

But if both readings are possible, how shall we decide what the sermon will be about? How do we determine where our exegesis of the text intersects with our understanding of our listeners? Many possibilities exist, no doubt, but so much of the pulpit pounding and moralizing one hears these days seems to forget that people already carry a load of guilt about their lives. Many, if not most, churchgoers are tuned into what Anne Lamott describes as a radio station with two messages playing in their ears. On the one side there are messages of confidence, reminders of giftedness and promise, but on the other side the never-ending stream of "self-loathing, the lists of all the things one doesn't do well, of all the mistakes one has made today and over an entire lifetime, the doubt," and so forth.[33]

"For the facing of this hour."

In late April of 2001, Davenport, Iowa, was devastated by floods. Joe M. Allbaugh, director of the Federal Emergency Management Agency (FEMA), promised a compassionate government response, but instead repeatedly scolded the city and its residents for their failure to build a permanent flood wall. At a time when people's homes had been destroyed, FEMA's top executive publicly scolded the residents for what they had failed to do. Not an isolated incident.

Similarly, week in and week out preachers pay lip service to God's love and unconditional acceptance only to place the real stress on how listeners have once again failed to live up to their potential. Rather than aim our homiletical telescopes toward God's stellar accomplishment, we have often settled for leaving the lens cap on and looking at our own reflection. As a result, the focus becomes too small and our content guilt-ridden. Such preaching is like those programs that distribute clean needles to junkies, promising no lectures, only to cluck the tongue and lecture them on morality; or like the police offering to receive unregistered handguns, no questions asked, then asking all sorts of questions about purchase and ownership. Make no mistake, there is a place in our preaching for challenge, just as that is part of the gospel. Is there also a place for grace?

In her fine essay on how she goes about giving birth to sermons, Linda Carolyn Loving tells about a mentor who once confided that most preachers have only one basic sermon in them. Most of us would have to concede it's true, that a subtle or not so subtle message informs all our sermons to a degree. Drawing on another mentor across the ages, Julian of Norwich, Loving discovered her "one sermon." She writes: "I believe that as preachers we are called to interpret and elicit the good in all, to see God in all. Not a Pollyanna preaching that excludes prophecy and pain, but preaching that is grounded in knowing, as Julian said, that ultimately 'all shall be well; and all will be well and thou shalt see thyself that all manner of thing shall be well.'"[34] May it be so!

Notes

1. These three constants, although debated at various times, can be traced back to John Broadus, *A Treatise on the Preparation and Delivery of Sermons*, rev. ed. (New York: Harper and Brothers, 1898), who noted four "special materials" of the sermon: explanation, illustration, application, and argumentation.
2. Robert N. Bellah et al., *Habits of the Heart: Individualism and Commitment in American Life*, rev. ed. (Berkeley: University of California Press, 1996), 32–33. Bellah and his colleagues note how Franklin actually marked his progress regarding certain virtues by means of a ledger sheet.
3. Robert Farrar Capon, *The Foolishness of Preaching: Proclaiming the Gospel against the Wisdom of the World* (Grand Rapids: Eerdmans, 1998), 39.
4. Dorothy C. Bass, ed., *Practicing Our Faith: A Way of Life for a Searching People* (San Francisco: Jossey-Bass, 1997); and Dorothy C. Bass and Miroslav Volf, eds., *Practicing Theology: Beliefs and Practices in Christian Life* (Grand Rapids: Eerdmans, 2001).
5. Harry Emerson Fosdick, "God of Grace and God of Glory," *Chalice Hymnal* (St. Louis: Chalice, 1995). Lines from this treasured hymn are used to organize this essay.
6. Christopher Morse, *Not Every Spirit: A Dogmatics of Christian Disbelief* (Valley Forge, Pa.: Trinity, 1994), 125. Emphases his.

7. Frederica Mathewes-Green, *At the Corner of East and Now: A Modern Life in Ancient Christian Orthodoxy* (New York: Jeremy P. Tarcher/Putnam, 1999), 146–47. Emphasis hers.

8. Karl Barth, *Homiletics*, trans. Geoffrey W. Bromiley and Donald E. Daniels (Louisville, Ky.: Westminster/John Knox, 1991), 47.

9. David S. Cunningham, *These Three Are One: The Practice of Trinitarian Theology* (Oxford: Blackwell, 1998), 101. Emphases his. In fairness to Barth, his latter preaching to the prisoners at Basel clearly demonstrates a pastoral concern for his listeners.

10. G. Lee Ramsey Jr., *Care-full Preaching* (St. Louis: Chalice, 2000), 80.

11. Thomas G. Long, *Whispering the Lyrics: Sermons for Lent and Easter* (Lima, Ohio: C.S.S. of Ohio, 1995), 28–29.

12. Marcus J. Borg, *Meeting Jesus Again for the First Time* (New York: HarperSan Francisco, 1994), chap. 6.

13. Frederick Buechner, *The Eyes of the Heart* (New York: HarperSan Francisco, 1999), 75.

14. James Sanders, "Torah and Christ," *Interpretation* 29 (July 1975): 381.

15. Herman G. Stuempfle Jr., *Preaching Law and Gospel* (Ramsey, N.J.: Sigler, 1990), 68. Emphasis his.

16. Capon, *Foolishness of Preaching*, 22. Emphasis his.

17. Wayne A. Meeks, *The Origins of Christian Morality: The First Two Centuries* (New Haven, Conn.: Yale University Press, 1993), 150–51.

18. Ibid., 5, 18, 74.

19. Victor Paul Furnish, *Theology and Ethics in Paul* (Nashville: Abingdon, 1968), 224–26. Emphasis his.

20. The issue is more complex than that of literary form. For instance, not all the narratives in Scripture are constitutive. Jesus' parable about the sheep and goats (Matt. 25:31–46) calls for social action on the part of believers even as Paul's letters sometimes remind readers of their baptismal status (Gal. 3:27–28). Some passages describe, others prescribe.

21. James W. McClendon Jr., *Systematic Theology: Ethics* (Nashville: Abingdon, 1986), 346.

22. Erskine Caldwell, *Tobacco Road* (New York: Grosset and Dunlap, 1932), 210. Emphases his. Thanks to Bill Stancil for pointing out this example to me.

23. Barbara Kingsolver, *The Poisonwood Bible* (New York: HarperPerennial, 1998), 26.

24. Thomas Merton, *The Seven Storey Mountain: An Autobiography of Faith* (San Diego: Harcourt and Brace, 1948), 81–82.

25. Marsha G. Witten, *All Is Forgiven: The Secular Message in American Protestantism* (Princeton, N.J.: Princeton University Press, 1993), 43–44.

26. Stuempfle, *Preaching Law and Gospel*, 34–35.

27. Frederick Buechner, "The Good Book as a Good Book," in *The Clown in the Belfry: Writings on Faith and Fiction* (San Francisco: HarperSanFrancisco, 1992), 44. In a recent article J. Clinton McCann Jr. ("The Hermeneutics of Grace," *Interpretation* 57 [January 2003]:5–6) cites Buechner on this very point. McCann concedes that while such an emphasis could result in oversimplification, it is a risk worth taking. Grace, he argues, "is the Bible's primary 'voice' or 'trajectory' against which all other voices or trajectories should be measured."

28. See Stuempfle, *Preaching Law and Gospel*, 20–33, who refuses to set one of these readings over against the other.

29. Ibid., 47.

30. James A. Sanders, *God Has a Story Too: Sermons in Context* (Philadelphia: Fortress, 1979), 17, who notes the *prophetic* nature of Scripture as well. See also Stuempfle, *Preaching Law and Gospel*, 26.

31. See Alyce McKenzie, *Preaching Biblical Wisdom in a Self-Help Society* (Nashville: Abingdon, 2002), who discusses the arduous task of preaching sound theology in a pop-culture obsessed with self-help.

32. Ramsey, *Care-full Preaching*, 74.

33. Anne Lamott, *Bird by Bird* (New York: Anchor, 1995), 116.

34. Linda Carolyn Loving, in *Birthing the Sermon: Women Preachers on the Creative Process*, ed. Jana Childers (St. Louis: Chalice, 2001), 103–4. Loving cites a one-woman drama by J. Janda, *Julian* (Englewood, N.J.: Pioneer Drama Service, 1979), 83.

Chapter Eight

Two Ships Passing in the Night

Cleophus J. LaRue

B lack preaching sprinted across the threshold into the twenty-first century in far better shape than much preaching in predominantly white churches. Though far from perfect, black preaching continues to be regarded in many circles as the most vibrant, imaginative, and communicatively effective preaching on the scene today. Over the past forty years, white homileticians have used such words as crisis, hemorrhaging, and lifeless to describe the preaching in their pulpits. Richard Eslinger was one among many who acknowledged that the preaching of the mainline churches was in crisis: "This awareness has been with us for a long time now, reducing pastoral morale and congregational fervor. But the way out, toward new effectiveness in preaching, is not yet clear."[1]

Even while taking note of the downward spiral in their own tradition, white homileticians saw in black preaching much that was admirable and attractive. In his volume entitled *Homiletic,* David Buttrick said, "I have been influenced by the Black homiletic tradition. All things considered, it is probable that the finest preaching in America today is Black."[2] In *The Bible in the Pulpit,* Leander Keck compared black and white preaching when he stated: "One could show rather easily that preaching has lost its centrality in most mainline white Protestant churches, although it has never lost its place in black Protestantism."[3]

Paul Scott Wilson characterized black preaching as arguably the strongest preaching tradition in the world, while Richard Lischer in a *Time* magazine feature said of the black church, "They remind us that the sermon is not a verbal essay but an oral performance of Scripture that includes the whole congregation."[4] Stephen Farris in *Preaching That Matters* made a case for analogical preaching, using as a prime example the sermon Martin Luther King Jr. preached in 1968 at the Mason Temple Church in Memphis, Tennessee, the night before he was assassinated. The exodus analogy that King employed of leading the people to the mountaintop, looking over, and seeing the promised land, stood out for Farris as an example of what was best in the analogical preaching he was attempting to describe.[5]

Paige Patterson, of the predominantly white Southern Baptist Convention, in an apparent nod to hyperbole, said of black preaching, "When it comes to rhetoric, the best Anglo preachers on their best days don't preach as well as a good black preacher on his worst day."[6] It was the black preaching of the civil rights movement that caught the ear of David James Randolph as he sensed a new preaching coming to birth under the banner of the New Homiletic. In *The Renewal of Preaching*, first published in 1969, Randolph said, "It is simply impossible to conceive of the present struggle for civil rights without the centrality of preachers and preaching in the movement. This central role is not one that came into being just recently. For long years preaching kept the soul of the [African American] alive, nourishing his spirit, enriching his vocabulary, and providing a means of expression and direction."[7]

When white homileticians engage in their critical reflection on homiletical theory and methodology, caveats and other exceptions must be inserted, for often it is the case that the reverse of what is being argued is true in black preaching. Again, Keck is helpful. Addressing the loss of confidence in mainline preaching, Keck notes,

> To begin with, many preachers today have lost confidence in the importance of preaching. . . . TV has made it ever more difficult for people to attend carefully to merely verbal communication, except perhaps for sports on radio. . . . This loss of attentiveness to verbal communication, to oral discourse, has eroded the place of the sermon. The black church is an exception, for there it is often customary for the congregation to participate in the preaching with "amens" and "right ons"; to some extent, the same must be conceded to white "Pentecostal" churches as well. It is the staid, sophisticated, mainline white Protestant churches that have been most affected. The preacher knows this quite well, and sometimes painfully; it has eroded the sense that preaching is important.[8]

The accolades being heaped on black preaching are not to suggest that this style of preaching is without its difficulties. An African American student minister said to a much lauded black preacher in Brooklyn, "Pastor, I have never heard a bad black sermon." To which the venerable old pastor replied, "Which rock have you been hiding under? I've heard lots of bad black sermons. I've preached quite a few of them myself." The seasoned pastor truly hit the nail on the head, for there is plenty in black preaching that is neither commendable nor worthy of emulation. One has only to tune in to Black Entertainment Television or a local cable TV channel to see questionable antics and unbridled heresy run amok in the black church.

All things considered, however, black preaching—if studied for more than its cosmetic effects of style and delivery, or its most widely known feature of celebration—has something of note to contribute to traditional homiletics in the twenty-first century. While there is no shortage of laudatory remarks regarding black preaching, the problem is that there is little or no substantive engagement of black preaching on behalf of those who speak so movingly of its potence and persuasive power. The dangers inherent in such nonengagement are legion.

First, there is the danger that two very fine preaching traditions—so intertwined in the complex of American religious life, faith, and history—stand the chance of passing each other as two ships in the night. Historian Mechal Sobel notes the manner in which blacks have historically influenced white religious perceptions, values, and identity. According to Sobel, "Although two world views existed, there was a deep symbiotic relatedness that must be explored if we are to understand either or both of them."[9]

Second, there is the problem of "disconnect" in preaching classes. In seminaries and divinity schools throughout America, because of our inability to engage one another to the enrichment of all, what is being taught by white homileticians seldom rises to the level of black expectations. Blacks are often more advanced in their preaching skills and generally bring more practical experience to the preaching classes than their white counterparts. Blacks, however, like most students, are in need of a sounder footing with respect to biblical, theological, and hermeneutical matters relative to preaching. Hearing little about what they know (their black preaching tradition) causes them to turn a deaf ear to what they need (the informed insight of traditional homiletics).

While it is clear that blacks have benefited from the theoretical and methodological insights of the major homileticians of the past century, what is equally clear, at least from a black perspective, is that this learning has often been a one-way street. What was being taught in the classrooms always came *to* blacks *from* the majority culture as if they (white homileticians) were the lone guardians of those standards by which we are to teach, gauge, and assess what constitutes good preaching. In preaching classes throughout America, twenty centuries of preaching could be taught without ever mentioning the name of a prominent black preacher. In some instances, white homileticians openly expressed their ignorance of black preaching and black preachers. And even more troubling, all too many indicated little desire to be exposed to what they clearly did not know.

In the waning years of the twentieth century, the name of Martin Luther King Jr. was invoked as an example of the finest in black preaching.[10] With rare exceptions, however, white homileticians seldom made any effort to look behind King in search of the tradition that shaped him and the long line of preachers he sought with such determination to emulate.[11] If, and when, they did get to blacks, the black preachers' limited contribution was "saved" for the end of the semester or the last day of the class, as if preaching done by blacks was an afterthought or an also-ran to the major white preaching story.[12]

Even now, as white homileticians search for new ways to reenergize their pulpits, a strong and vibrant preaching tradition—born in part in their own house—goes largely unrecognized in their midst. While it is not my desire to turn white preachers into black preachers or vice versa, I do believe both traditions can profit from one another's strengths and weaknesses as our multidimensional, diverse Christian church moves into its fifth century of preaching on American shores.

Where to Begin?

Some of the interchange can begin simply by questioning why something that has clearly fallen on hard times in the white preaching tradition still works in black preaching. For example, Fred Craddock's dismissal of deductive preaching and the three-point sermon. Craddock rightly argued that not only the content of preaching, but the method of preaching is fundamentally a theological consideration. He noted that there were basically two directions in which thought moved: deductive and inductive. Simply stated, he said, "Deductive movement is from the general truth to the particular application or experience while induction is the reverse. Homiletically, deduction means stating the thesis, breaking it down into points or sub-theses, explaining and illustrating these points, and applying them to the particular situations of the hearers."[13]

He dismissed the three-point sermon as outdated, out of touch with the pew, and ill-suited to address modern-day listeners with its deductive approach, authoritarian stance, and deliberate naming of what the listener should take away from the sermon today. In the deductive sermon, argued Craddock, there is no democracy, no dialogue, no listening by the speaker, no contributing by the hearer. He said deductive preaching was flat, lacking in imagination, and created passivity in the listeners. If the congregation is on the team, he said, "it is as javelin catcher."[14] Craddock struck a nerve with white preachers, conservative and mainline alike, throughout America. He also had a great impact on the teaching of homiletics in seminaries and divinity schools in the last quarter of the twentieth century.

So strong was Craddock's broadside against the deductive "three-point sermon and a poem," that when I arrived as a student at Princeton Theological Seminary in the 1980s, the perception that the three-point sermon was long since history hung heavily in the air. That perception struck me as quite strange, since I'd just heard a three-point sermon the day before in one of New York City's premiere black churches. Immediately in my mind there was a disconnect between what white homileticians were espousing and what was going on in the black church. Again, Craddock had valid reasons for moving away from that type of sermonic form in many white churches—the changing nature of language, the turn to the listener, a fear of concreteness, the inability to name God's presence in the lived experience of the human situation, and so forth.

In the black church, however, the deductive, three-point sermon simply did not have the same disastrous effects it apparently did in some white congregations. This idea of a boring preacher, or an overly authoritarian preacher thundering broadsides to a disconnected, discontented audience is not what the three-point sermon wrought in the best of black preaching. Not then, not now. The three-point sermon in the black church is clothed in imagination, humor, playful engagement, running narrative, picturesque speech, and audible participation on the part of the congregation. Thus, it is not the three-point sermon that is out, but rather it is the *boring* three-point sermon that must go. Should blacks be exposed to other forms of preaching? Of course! But must we throw the three-point baby out with the bath in order to achieve this? I think not!

The differences between black and white churches regarding the three-point sermon and deductive preaching are striking, and thus worthy of investigation. Why is it believed to fail in one church while it flies in the other? What can we teach one another about its use or lack thereof? In fairness to Craddock, to read him is to understand that he is speaking primarily to white preachers, trying valiantly to lift their preaching out of the sermonic doldrums. However, when Craddock's method is taught in seminaries those who teach it do not always specify that his concerns are addressed primarily to whites. That oversight is where the disconnect comes to the fore. Blacks who have had positive experiences with the deductive, three-point sermon feel unaddressed and left out of the homiletical loop. Or they are left with the uneasy feeling that the homiletics teacher is scratching where the black church is simply not itching. Some would have us move away from the three-point sermon simply for the sake of novelty. In the black community, however, there is too much at stake in the daily struggle to survive to try the latest fad simply for the sake of difference. It's not variety per se that blacks seek in the preached word, it is the ring of truth heard even above the din of the various forms and homiletic constructs.

Another example of differences between black and traditional homiletics is Buttrick's understanding of sermon introductions. In *Homiletic*, Buttrick said of introductions that while they give "focus," they should never give away the sermon ahead of time. He added, "A good rule for preachers as for poker players: Never tip your hand."

> Introductions should not be too long inasmuch as getting into focus can be accomplished rather quickly. So, as a general guideline, introductions may run between seven and twelve sentences in length. The sentence count is not arbitrary. An introduction can scarcely function in less than seven sentences. At the same time, after more than a dozen sentences congregational impatience will usually set in.[15]

Such guidelines for novice preachers are sure to be helpful in some situations, even if debatable, but to state it simply: one must include some additional criteria for introductions in black preaching. In black churches it is understood that the preacher is going to take his or her time in the introduction of the sermon. In a complete reversal of Buttrick's admonition, not infrequently some blacks actually state up front what they're going to talk about, and the people still listen.[16] Hard-and-fast rules about length, timing, and retaining elements of surprise are not strictly enforced in the black church. Why are black congregations willing to give their preachers more time? Are there different listening expectations? Is the congregation more willing to hear a lengthy introduction if they believe the preacher will make it worth their while before the sermon has ended?

I believe there are different levels of listening and expectation in black congregations. These levels are cyclical, and not linear. This differentiation gives the preacher more time than would be allowed in the average white church. First, more time is allowed in setting up the sermon because the preaching event is a much-anticipated, central component in the black worship experience. If neoorthodox theologian Karl Barth is right in his assertion about what the Reformers took from us—everything but the Bible—allowing ample time for the preaching of the Word is in indeed a theological act.[17] Second, the cyclical levels of listening allow the preacher more than one chance to lose a congregation and pick them up again. Multiple chances to reignite a congregation's interest are apparently less tolerated in white churches.

Seldom is a sermon in the black church completely written off by the listeners at the outset, poor introduction notwithstanding. In fact, "Take your time, preacher," is the most common refrain heard in the congregation at the beginning of the sermon.[18] Levels of listening allow the parishioners to gain something from the sermon even when it violates every established rule of thumb relative to the introduction, body, and close. There is a sense in which the listener simply changes gears in order to accommodate the preacher's level of communication and clarity.

The first level is what I call *high alert*. This is the highest level of expectation. Oddly enough, while it usually occurs at the beginning of a sermon according to white homileticians, sometimes it can actually take place near the end of a black sermon. High alert is that point in the sermon where listeners are willing to give the preacher a chance to address them in a meaningful, coherent, and challenging manner. They are listening attentively, attempting to figure out how the word of God has addressed them that day and what claim is being made on their lives. Some preachers can hold the congregation's attention from beginning to end, while others need time to hit their stride. The listening gears in the black church give preachers and listeners time to adjust to one another's communicative style.

The second level is *pearls without a string*. When the black listeners make up in their minds that the preacher lacks coherence, logical flow, and initial purposeful encounter, they don't stop listening, they simply listen with different expectations. They change gears. The listeners decide to retrieve as much as possible from the sermon through the gathering of meaningful pearls here and there. Pearls are ideas and concepts that stand alone, unrelated, or at least disconnected in the listener's mind to other parts of the sermon. But they are helpful, nonetheless, to the listener because they offer some word that is meaningful, enlightening, or that resonates with their lived experience. The listeners string together whatever word of truth, illustration, or meaningful phrase they can in order to find something of worth in the sermon.

Third is *broken pieces*. This level represents a last-ditch effort on the part of the listener to salvage something of worth from the sermon. All hope is gone for some clearly defined, controlling thought. Even pearls without a string are in short supply. The listener is reduced to a search for that *one* thing that will bear the imprimatur of the sacred. It can be a line of truth, a slice of life, a well-timed cliché, or a sidebar illustration totally unrelated to anything concerning the title, focus, or announced intent of the sermon. Sometimes it is the preacher's manner of speech and affable personality that end up carrying the day: "Well, at least he was well spoken and friendly." Which is to say, they found grace in his willingness to be present for God, though not necessarily in his preaching about God. Broken pieces point to a bit of something here and a part of something there. The listener is determined to ride some meaningful piece of truth to the shore of understanding.

Fourth is *clock watching*. At this stage of listening the clock is speaking louder than the preacher. The listeners have given up all hope that the preacher will have anything meaningful to say. They simply sit tight, content to run out the clock. If sympathetic, they give the preacher the benefit of the doubt, attributing the ineffectiveness to a busy week or a crowded schedule. If not, there is inward disgust and silent anguish at the poor performance of the preacher, who was given every chance from beginning to end to salvage the sermon. These are the four levels at work throughout the sermon. The employment of any level at any given moment helps the black parishioner retrieve something from even the most poorly constructed, poorly delivered sermon.

Is a sermon that requires the changing of so many gears the ideal sermon? Absolutely not! Do parishioners have a right to expect more? Certainly! And on most Sundays they get more. However, even on off Sundays the black church is determined to hear a word from God. Their desire to salvage something from every sermon is actually biblical in its roots and encouraging in its consistency:

> For as the rain and the snow come down from heaven,
>   and do not return there until they have watered the earth,
> making it bring forth and sprout,
>   giving seed to the sower and bread to the eater,

so shall my word be that goes out from my mouth;
>   it shall not return to me empty,
> but it shall accomplish that which I purpose,
>   and succeed in the thing for which I sent it.

Isa. 55:10–11

It is this text and its promise that keeps black congregants listening even when they have every right to tune the preacher out. To dismiss the preacher out of hand at the introduction simply doesn't allow enough time for these traditional levels of listening to kick in. To institute hard-and-fast rules is to suggest that the black parishioner has only one level of listening—*high alert!* It also suggests low levels of expectation.

These are just two examples of ways the two traditions could be helpful to one another. Eugene Lowry's reversal and element of surprise, Paul Scott Wilson's four pages of the sermon, Thomas Long's brainstorming and claim of the text, Charles Campbell's understanding of what it means to "preach Jesus," and the traditional understanding of what constitutes the gospel and/or proclamation are all open for discussion and could profit from a healthy engagement with the black preaching tradition.[19] And vice versa. All these scholars have made valuable contributions to contemporary homiletics. To highlight bits and pieces of their works may seem unfair. That is not my aim. These critiques are not intended to be exhaustive; rather it is hoped that they will foster more discussion between the traditions, not less.

How Blacks Learn to Preach

Another striking difference between black preaching and white homiletics is the manner in which blacks learn to preach. Separate and apart from matters of form, structure, content, and style, the entire black approach to the teaching of preaching differs markedly from the established pedagogy in traditional homiletics. Why is it the case that many blacks continue to learn to preach primarily through *emulation* of accomplished preachers they have come to admire? To emulate is not to copy, but rather to set a standard of achievement by which one gauges one's own preaching ability and advancement. Does learning by listening suggest that blacks are anti-intellectual and thus unmindful of the importance of gaining a seminary-trained foundation in preaching?

The black church believes that teaching people to preach is fundamentally an ecclesial act, and thus by its very nature a pedagogical function that the church cannot relegate to the academy alone. If indeed the Scriptures belong to the church, then the church cannot abdicate its responsibility in the guidance of those who will explicate those Scriptures in the name of the church. That blacks continue to learn to preach by listening to those whom they admire and respect—who are for the most part accomplished preachers who have received the approbation of the churchgoing public— is a theological act of the highest order.

That the black church continues to call and promote those who have been trained to preach in this manner is, I believe, its way of saying that it will have a determining voice and a controlling hand in the formation of those who advance through its ranks. This is especially true in the present era, when modern biblical scholarship has sought in many ways to relegate the church's understanding of Scripture to "interpretive irrelevance."[20] For the most part, whites in mainline and High Church congregations are declared fit to preach once they have successfully completed the degree requirements of a bona fide theological institution and passed the basic exams required by their particular judicatories. Many are not even eligible to be considered for the top positions in churches until this part of their education has been successfully completed. Thus they come to their charges, for the most part, with very little preaching experience.

In this respect blacks have the advantage over their white counterparts, for they have been trying their hand at preaching under the watchful eye of a local fellowship or judicatory since the announcement of their call. The black church, while not nearly as adamant about formal training as it should be, does not view such training as a replacement for its role in the formation of the preacher. It continues to administer its very vital function of shaping, directing, and teaching the newly called preacher of the gospel.

In many black churches, and in some white churches as well (some Baptist, Methodist, and Pentecostal, to name a few), the preacher is encouraged to go to school, but the lack of formal training does not prevent one from taking on preaching assignments and responsibilities. While the black preacher is clearly better off with the formal tools of investigation and the in-depth theological insight one receives through the successful completion of a certified theological program, the black church sees its role in the training of the minister as equally important.

Might not there be room in the academy for the surefire experience of seasoned mentors alongside the formal training that is currently taught? Young preachers need exposure to experienced pastors who can pass on to them not merely a skill, but a way of life, a preaching "habitus," if you will. We can no longer assume that those who sit before us in preaching class come to us with a good foundation in the life, witness, and ministerial practices of the church. It is here that the seasoned pastor, on the craft in the stream, can be of great help to those who are just beginning to try their hands and their hearts at preaching.

In many white churches one is declared fit to preach through *certification*. In the black church one is declared fit to preach through *demonstration*. In the former you have to show that you have been appropriately exposed to the fundamentals of preaching, while in the latter you have to show that you actually have some proficiency in the preaching act itself.

Blacks are coming more and more to appreciate and require that their preachers be formally trained in accredited theological institutions. And rightly so! The church benefits greatly from the minister who has experienced the formal study of a theological seminary or divinity school. The preacher's overall ministry is strengthened when he or she has been exposed, in a formal way, to biblical studies, church history, theology, and practical theology. Such study makes for a more grounded preacher, and it creates in the person of the preacher an enhanced capacity for theological vision and discernment. That said, however, a degree alone will seldom get the minister a job in a black church. Ministers have to demonstrate, or at least show promise, to pulpit committees and congregations alike that they can carry the weight of the pulpit. Most black churches continue to put preaching skills high on their must-have list when searching for a pastor.

What Is Black Preaching?

Granted, even while attempting to make a case for a more serious engagement with the particulars of black preaching, I must acknowledge that blacks themselves are not in agreement as to how we define *black preaching*. (Neither is traditional homiletics of one mind about its preaching.) Nor are blacks in agreement on a unified definition of *the black church*. Many among us say there's no such entity. When white religious bodies with significant African American memberships are included, blacks belong to over two hundred denominations in the United States alone.[21] And as of 1997, churchgoing blacks in America claimed to have over twenty-five million members in more than sixty-three thousand congregations.[22] While most blacks belong to predominantly black denominations, a sizable number are in predominantly white denominations and would take exception to being left out of the definition of what constitutes *the* traditional black church.

C. Eric Lincoln and Lawrence Mamiya in their seminal study on the black church maintained that, in general, any black Christian person is included in the black church if he or she is a member of a black congregation, denomination notwithstanding. However, in their book *The Black Church in the African-American Experience* they chose to limit their operational definition of "the black church" to the seven independent, historic, and totally black-controlled denominations: three Methodist conferences, three Baptist conventions, and the Church of God in Christ.[23] Many would say their operational definition of the black church is too narrow.

With respect to the question of what constitutes "black preaching," there is a very powerful and settled school of thought among black preachers that says there is no such thing as black preaching per se, with its own specific characteristics and distinctive traits. Those who maintain this view say there are black preachers who preach, but they don't preach black, they simply preach the gospel. Chief among the proponents of this position was the late Samuel DeWitt Proctor, pastor emeritus of the Abyssinian Baptist Church in New York and professor of the Martin Luther King Chair in Ethics at Rutgers University.

Proctor, though not anti–black preaching, simply believed there was too much diversity within the tradition historically or as presently constructed to make accurate generalizations. Proctor observed that African American preaching demonstrated the same diversity as other forms of American Christianity and should not be characterized by style of delivery or theological assumptions.[24] His books on preaching were simply titled *Preaching about Crises in the Community* and *The Certain Sound of the Trumpet*. His autobiography was titled *The Substance of Things Hoped For*.[25] Although he cowrote a volume of sermons with William Watley titled *Sermons from the Black Pulpit*, he was uneasy with the characterization of black preaching as a distinct body of literature to be studied and reflected upon.[26]

Others in black religious circles, while not as outspoken as Proctor, were also hesitant to style their works on preaching as peculiarly or uniquely black. Gardner Taylor, regarded by many as the dean of black preachers, titled his Lyman Beecher lectures in book form simply: *How Shall They Preach*.[27] Taylor quotes more European preachers than he does black preachers or black homileticians in his book. Another black preacher/homiletician who comes to mind is James Forbes, and his work *The Holy Spirit and Preaching*.[28] Forbes has been described as the first contemporary "crossover" preacher in his ministry to the multiracial, multidenominational Riverside Church in New York City—crossover meaning he was intentionally seeking to have broad appeal to as wide and diverse an audience as possible.

Even the black neo-Pentecostals and evangelicals on the order of T. D. Jakes and Bishop Paul Morton have made an effort to steer clear of racial designations in many of their published works. Some out-and-out deny any such characteristics exist, while others simply move away from explicit references in an effort to broaden their appeal.

There are those, however, who believe there are sufficient characteristics in this style of proclamation to warrant the title "black preaching." This is not to suggest that the things that go on in this style are unique to black preaching or done by all black preachers, but it is to say that when taken together they come to the fore with such clarity and presence that one would not err in saying that these are some of the things you find repeatedly in the best of black preaching.

Characteristics of Black Preaching

The multiple characteristics of black preaching are cited here more as a starting place for those interested in learning more about the black preaching tradition than as a stopping point for what blacks have to contribute to the homiletical discussion. William B. McClain in *The Renewal of Sunday Worship* lists as characteristics of black preaching: biblical emphasis, prophetic preaching, a poetic style, dialogue, preaching that is declarative rather than suggestive, and preaching that is life-situational and contains some element of hope.[29]

James Earl Massey in *The Responsible Pulpit* listed five insights from the black preaching tradition with respect to the sermon: The sermon is *functional* in that it is always regarded as a means to an end. It is *festive* in that it deals with concrete life and aims to be an invitation to joy even in the midst of sorrow and struggle. It is *communal* in that it must aid the sense of group life. It is *radical* in that it seeks to confront the hearers in the very depths of their beings with the issues of life. And finally, said Massey, the black sermon is *climactic* in that it seeks some type of celebratory close to make an impression on the hearers.[30]

Henry Mitchell, the foremost proponent of black preaching over the past three decades, made "celebration" the cornerstone of his homiletic.[31] In a later essay Mitchell listed three chief characteristics of preaching in traditional African American churches. First was intonation or "whooping," a chanting or singsong style of delivery in black preaching. Second was spontaneity, by which he means the ability to respond to the movement of the

Spirit among preacher and congregation and to express deep feeling without shame. Third was the basic structure of the sermon, which Mitchell characterized as imaginative, narrative, and prone to generate an experiential encounter.[32]

Evans Crawford and Thomas Troeger cited participatory proclamation, or what some refer to as call-and-response, as a distinctive feature of African American preaching. In their work, those unfamiliar with the tradition were able to gain some insight into the antiphonal nature of the black worship experience as well as being able to see how preacher and people give life and encouragement to one another at the preaching hour. The authors draw on five distinct phrases to demonstrate how participatory proclamation is brought to life in the black church ("Help him, Lord!" "Well!" "That's alright!" "Amen!" "Glory hallelujah!").[33]

Others have characterized a high regard for Scripture, a creative use of language, an appeal to emotions, and the granting of a certain authority or freedom to black preachers as significant characteristics. In an earlier work I, too, made an attempt to list the characteristics foundational to this style of preaching. I argued that distinctiveness was not simply in the black style of delivery or manner of preaching, but more importantly in our content.

When blacks respond enthusiastically in their worship settings to the preached word, they are not merely caught up in the emotions of the moment. They are, in part, responding to content shaped by a very powerful oral delivery. Among the distinctives in matters of content, I cited a biblical hermeneutic of a sovereign God who acts powerfully on the part of the disinherited, and five realms or domains of experience into which and out of which blacks are shaped by the gospel and their lived situations.[34]

All such characteristics can only be described as identifying different parts of an immense task. They are, however, important places to begin the interactive quest. Moreover, substantive books on black preaching and books on preaching written by blacks abound, and they simply await engagement by the traditional homileticians. To the benefit of all, some have already begun this process of intersecting and interacting with black preaching. The act of preaching and the teaching of preaching can only be the better for it.[35]

To Begin Again

American Protestant preaching will surely be strengthened by the enhanced reflection and the continuous interaction of these two very fine preaching traditions. In the twenty-first century it can no longer be a one-way preaching street, with white homileticians on the sending end and black preachers on the receiving end. In the immediate future, seminaries and divinity schools will need to rethink staffing needs, not just so that blacks can have someone in preaching who understands their tradition but also so that whites and others might be exposed in a formal way to the best insights of a vibrant preaching tradition of long standing in their own midst. Those who resist and refuse the imminent developments coming to us could find themselves speaking into a smaller and smaller circle.

The parameters of homiletics are ever expanding, and contextuality will be the name of the game in the years to come. Hispanics, Asian Americans, Native Americans, and others will have much to contribute to this discussion. A healthy appreciation of and lively exchange between all homiletic traditions will make for stronger preachers irrespective of ethnicity, gender, regional differences, and denominational ties. The teaching of preaching in the future, if it is to be effective, will have to reflect the broad and rich diversity of the global village that is now so clearly upon us and so much a part of who we are. Celebrating and building on our diversity are among the things most needful in our preaching today. If, indeed, all roads lead to preaching, then homileticians should take the lead in showing the church a more excellent way.

Notes

1. Richard Eslinger, *A New Hearing: Living Options in Homiletic Method* (Nashville: Abingdon, 1987), 11.
2. David Buttrick, *Homiletic* (Philadelphia: Fortress, 1987), 469.
3. Leander Keck, *The Bible in the Pulpit* (Nashville: Abingdon, 1978), 15.
4. David Van Biema and Nadia Mustafa, "How Much Does Preaching Matter?" *Time*, September 17, 2001, 55.
5. Stephen Farris, *Preaching That Matters* (Louisville, Ky.: Westminster John Knox, 1998), 18–19.
6. David Van Biema, "America's Best: Spirit Raiser," *Time*, September 17, 2001, 53.
7. David James Randolph, *The Renewal of Preaching* (Philadelphia: Fortress, 1969), 2.
8. Keck, 40.
9. Mechal Sobel, *The World They Made Together: Black and White Values in Eighteenth-Century Virginia* (Princeton, N.J.: Princeton University Press, 1987), 11. See also Nathan O. Hatch, *The Democratization of American Christianity* (New Haven, Conn.: Yale University Press, 1989); and Donald G. Mathews, *Religion in the Old South* (Chicago: University of Chicago Press, 1977).
10. James W. Cox, ed., *The Twentieth Century Pulpit* (Nashville: Abingdon, 1978), 115–23. Justo González, in his critique of this work, rightly notes that a rapid glance at the list of contributors shows that they are all male, and that almost all of them are white. See González, *Liberation Preaching* (Nashville: Abingdon, 1980), 46. Had the editor sought a more inclusive list of black preachers and sermons, he could have read the works of

such nineteenth- and early-twentieth-century greats as Alexander Crummell, *The Greatness of Christ and Other Sermons* (New York: Thomas Whittaker, 1882); *Africa and America: Addresses and Discourses* (New York: Negro Universities, 1891); Carter G. Woodson, ed., *The Works of Francis J. Grimke*, Special Collections, Princeton Theological Seminary; J. W. Hood, *The Negro in the Christian Pulpit* (Raleigh, N.C.: Edwards, Broughton, 1884); C. S. Smith, *Sermons Delivered by Bishop Daniel A. Payne* (Nashville: Publishing House of the A.M.E. Sunday School Union, 1888); and Theodore S. Boone, *"Lord! Lord!": Special Occasion Sermons and Addresses of Dr. L. K. Williams* (Nashville: Historical Commission, National Baptist Convention, 1942).

11. The notable exceptions are Keith D. Miller, *Voice of Deliverance: The Language of Martin Luther King Jr. and Its Sources* (New York: Free Press, 1992); Richard Lischer, *The Preacher King: Martin Luther King Jr. and the Word That Moved America* (New York: Oxford University Press, 1995); Richard L. Eslinger, *The Web of Preaching* (Nashville: Abingdon, 2002); and L. Susan Bond, *Contemporary African American Preaching: Diversity in Theory and Style* (St. Louis: Chalice, 2003). Stephen Farris, Leonora Tisdale, and Paul Scott Wilson, among others, have sought to incorporate black preachers and homileticians into their works on preaching.

12. Even books on great preaching published in the twentieth century were slow about including the sermons of prominent historical African American preachers. Clyde E. Fant Jr. and William M. Pinson Jr., eds., *Twenty Centuries of Great Preaching: An Encyclopedia of Preaching* (Waco: Word, 1971), cited the names of John Jasper and Martin Luther King Jr. in their multivolume set. Warren W. Wiersbe, ed., *Treasury of the World's Great Sermons* (Grand Rapids: Kregel, 1977), published the sermons of no recognizable black preachers from the early beginnings of Christianity through the twentieth century. Not even a sermon by Martin Luther King Jr. was able to make his list. To Wiersbe's credit, he widened his circle and came in later years to have an appreciation for black preaching with the publication of his coauthored conversations on preaching with African American pastor E. K. Bailey. See E. K. Bailey and Warren Wiersbe, *Preaching in Black and White: What We Can Learn from Each Other* (Grand Rapids: Zondervan, 2003).

13. Fred B. Craddock, *As One Without Authority*, rev. ed. (St. Louis: Chalice, 2001), 45.

14. Ibid., 46.

15. Buttrick, *Homiletic*, 86.

16. See Cheryl Sanders's essay "Preaching with Passion," in *Power in the Pulpit*, ed. Cleophus J. LaRue (Louisville, Ky.: Westminster John Knox, 2002), 117–28.

17. Karl Barth, *The Word of God and the Word of Man*, trans. Douglas Horton (Gloucester, Mass.: Peter Smith, 1978), 114.

18. For a more detailed analysis of the call-and-response dynamic in the black worship setting, see Evans E. Crawford with Thomas H. Troeger, *The Hum: Call and Response in African American Preaching* (Nashville: Abingdon, 1995).

19. Eugene L. Lowry, *The Homiletical Plot: The Sermon as Narrative Art Form* (Atlanta: John Knox, 1980); Paul Scott Wilson, *The Four Pages of the Sermon: A Guide to Biblical Preaching* (Nashville, Ky.: Abingdon, 1999); Thomas G. Long, *The Witness of Preaching* (Louisville, Ky.: Westminster/John Knox, 1989); Charles L. Campbell, *Preaching Jesus: New Directions for Homiletics in Hans Frei's Postliberal Theology* (Grand Rapids: Eerdmans, 1997); Gerhard O. Forde, *Theology Is for Proclamation* (Minneapolis: Fortress, 1990); and

Edward Farley, *Practicing Gospel: Unconventional Thoughts on the Church's Ministry* (Louisville, Ky.: Westminster John Knox, 2003).

20. James J. Buckley and David S. Yeago, eds., *Knowing the Triune God: The Work of the Spirit in the Practices of the Church* (Grand Rapids: Eerdmans, 2001), 49–93.

21. Wardell J. Payne, ed., *Directory of African American Religious Bodies* (Washington, D.C.: Howard University, 1991), 21–47, 199–216; and Larry G. Murphy, J. Gordon Melton, and Gary L. Ward, eds., *Encyclopedia of African American Religions* (New York: Garland, 1993), xx. The *Encyclopedia* lists some 341 black religious organizations.

22. Anthony B. Pinn, *The Black Church in the Post–Civil Rights Era* (Maryknoll, N.Y.: Orbis, 2002), 35.

23. C. Eric Lincoln and Lawrence H. Mamiya, *The Black Church in the African American Experience* (Durham, N.C.: Duke University Press, 1990), 1.

24. Bond, *African American Preaching*, 44.

25. Samuel D. Proctor, *Preaching about Crises in the Community* (Philadelphia: Westminster, 1988); *The Certain Sound of the Trumpet: Crafting a Sermon of Authority* (Valley Forge, Pa.: Judson, 1994); *The Substance of Things Hoped For: A Memoir of African-American Faith* (New York: G. P. Putnam's Sons, 1995).

26. Samuel D. Proctor and William D. Watley, *Sermons from the Black Pulpit* (Valley Forge, Pa.: Judson, 1984).

27. Gardner C. Taylor, *How Shall They Preach* (Elgin, Ill.: Progressive Baptist Publishing House, 1977).

28. James Forbes Jr., *The Holy Spirit and Preaching* (Nashville: Abingdon, 1989).

29. William B. McClain, "African-American Preaching," in *The Renewal of Sunday Worship*, ed. Robert E. Webber (Nashville: StarSong, 1993), 315–19.

30. James Earl Massey, *The Responsible Pulpit* (Anderson, Ind.: Warner, 1974), 101–11.

31. Henry Mitchell, *Black Preaching* (San Francisco: Harper and Row, 1979); *Experience and Celebration in Preaching* (Nashville: Abingdon, 1990).

32. Henry Mitchell, "African-American Preaching," in *Concise Encyclopedia of Preaching*, ed. William H. Willimon and Richard Lischer (Louisville, Ky.: Westminster John Knox, 1995), 3–9.

33. Crawford and Troeger, *The Hum*, 13.

34. Cleophus J. LaRue, *The Heart of Black Preaching* (Louisville, Ky.: Westminster John Knox, 2000).

35. For works on black preaching and works written by black preachers other than those referenced earlier, see: Kelly Miller Smith, *Social Crisis Preaching* (Macon, Ga.: Mercer University, 1983); Olin P. Moyd, *The Sacred Art: Preaching and Theology in the African American Tradition* (Valley Forge, Pa.: Judson, 1995); Miles Jones, *Preaching Papers: The Hampton and Virginia Union Lectures* (New York: MLK Fellows, 1995); Warren H. Stewart, *Interpreting God's Word in Black Preaching* (Valley Forge, Pa.: Judson, 1984); James H. Harris, *Preaching Liberation* (Minneapolis: Fortress, 1993); Bruce A. Rosenberg, *Can These Bones Live? The Art of the American Folk Preacher* (New York: Oxford University Press, 1970; Frank A. Thomas, *They Like to Never Quit Praisin' the Lord: The Role of Celebration in Preaching* (New York: Pilgrim, 1997); Gerald L. Davis, *I Got the Word in Me and I Can Sing It, You Know: A Study of the Performed African-American Sermon* (Philadelphia: University of Pennsylvania Press, 1985); Bettye Collier-Thomas, *Daughters of Thunder: Black Women Preachers and Their Sermons, 1850–1979* (Hoboken,

N.J.: John Wiley, 1997); Katie G. Cannon, *Teaching Preaching: Isaac Rufus Clark and Black Sacred Rhetoric* (New York: Continuum, 2002); Marvin McMickle, *Preaching to the Black Middle Class* (Valley Forge, Pa.: Judson, 2000); and Teresa Fry Brown, *Weary Throats and New Songs: Black Women Preaching God's Word* (Nashville: Abingdon, 2003). For two excellent pieces where blacks and whites are in conversation with one another see: Bailey and Wiersbe, *Preaching in Black and White*, and Brian K. Blount and Gary W. Charles, *Preaching Mark in Two Voices* (Louisville, Ky.: Westminster John Knox, 2002).

Chapter Nine

No News Is Bad News

Thomas G. Long

W hat is the matter with preaching today? Trying to answer that question is a little like flushing out a covey of quail. One hardly knows where to shoot. What's gone wrong with preaching? Is it content, style, language, purpose, relevance, delivery? All of the above? Everybody has an opinion, a pet peeve, about sermons—at least everybody who still cares enough to raise a critique. Sermons are boring or sensationalist, trivial or pompous, irrelevant or trendy, too caught up in "Bible speak" or not biblical enough, too long or too short, too worldly or too remote, and on and on. Even the Beatles had a little sport with the futile and lonely Father McKenzie, writing sermons "no one would hear."

There is nothing new, of course, in carping about sermons. In the face of all this criticism, adding yet another gibe at poor preachers and their sermons seems unnecessary, excessive, a little like piling on. As a preacher myself, I am well aware that this preaching business is not simple stuff. Think about the task: week after week, preachers attempt to climb Mount Everest–sized texts and to scale the rock face of Trinitarian theology in front of occasionally distracted, often sleepy, sometimes diminishing, always media-saturated congregations. To carp at these preachers because their pitons were loose or suggesting that they suffered oxygen deprivation or that they lost their nerve near the summit seems greatly to miss the point. The fact that they get back up the next week and try this nigh impossible climb again is a wondrous and beautiful thing. Who else in our culture is expected to commit public hermeneutics every seven days?

Fosdick Revisited

When the notable preacher and teacher Harry Emerson Fosdick, who eventually became the first pastor of the Riverside Church in New York, wrote his classic 1928 *Harper's Magazine* article "What Is the Matter with Preaching?" he was not simply adding his two cents to the unceasing carping of sermon critics. Fosdick was not niggling over this or that little homiletical flaw or foible. Rather Fosdick was insisting that the essential conditions for the hearing of preaching had changed. He was reading the seismograph of his age, warning his fellow preachers that while they slumbered the earth had shaken and shifted beneath them. Preachers, he argued, were assuming one frame of reference for hearers—namely, that they were interested in the world of the Bible, that indeed they lived in that world and were fascinated with its ideas, characters, and themes—while the truth was that this world had collapsed in ruins in the night. People now lived, claimed Fosdick, not in a world of the grand biblical narratives and overarching Christian myths, but rather in a smaller world of personal spiritual "problems," puzzling religious contradictions, and troubling doubts. Writing in the roaring '20s, Fosdick accused his colleagues of preaching Strauss waltzes while the world was into jazz.

Are we again at such a moment? Are we once more at the point where preaching must do more than adjust the jib, when a whole new tack is needed, when, like Fosdick, we must ask what has gone wrong with the soul of preaching? If we are, it is tempting to say that the problem with preaching today is that we took Fosdick's advice entirely too seriously. One way to read Fosdick's essay is to say that he was perhaps the first preacher in the world to be self-consciously alert to the appearance of the highly individualistic religious consumer so familiar to all of us today. Sixty years before Harry and Mary Seeker would make their appearance in the church growth literature, Fosdick spotted their grandparents lurking in his congregation, hiding their free-range spirituality behind starched collars and feather hats.

While the run-of-the-mill preachers were blindly ignoring the changes in the pews and soldiering on with preaching as usual, either expounding texts from the Bible or sonorously exploring some theme such as "divorce" or "America's Nicaraguan policy," Fosdick looked out at the congregation and saw not parishioners, but *customers*. The effective preacher, he argued, "is delivering the goods that the community has a right to expect from the pulpit as much as it has a right to expect shoes from a cobbler." And what was the purpose of preaching? The "only justifiable aim" of a sermon, in

Fosdick's view, was to help people "solve their spiritual problems." The preacher was supposed to name a personal problem that the listeners were vitally concerned about and then throw some light on it. Within a couple of paragraphs, the listeners were to snap to attention with the recognition that the preacher was up there talking about something of real interest to them.

Fosdick was, of course, one of the greatest preachers ever, and we are right to remain awed by his powers, but confined to this popular essay and taken at face value, his views on the purpose of preaching are a disaster. Liberal and modernist that he was, Fosdick would be shocked by the charge that he was godfather to the megachurch movement. Nevertheless, his consumer-oriented homiletics, with its pragmatic apple pie recipe of marketing and psychotherapy, has now found a comfy home in many an American jumbo "cathedral" and temple of the current zeitgeist. Fosdick's method of preaching begins, in effect, by asking the hearers, "What's on your mind today? What's troubling your soul?" That works well and summons magnificent preaching as long as soaring concerns like doubt, joy, faith, and hope are on their minds, but the whole process tends to go to seed when time management, personal investing, effective parenting, and self-esteem are deemed the big spiritual challenges of the day. Fosdick saw the congregation as a collection of spiritual consumers, but he was thinking Tiffany's. He never dreamed that the market was going Wal-Mart on us. Score a point for Karl Barth here, who once warned that "the Bible does not always answer our questions, but sometimes calls our questions into question."

At another level, though, it's a long way from Riverside to Willow Creek, and Fosdick deserves (though he does not really need) at least a mild word of defense. Against the backdrop of preaching that had lost its zest, preaching that was abstract and remote, preaching that was obsessed with the need to explain texts and expound doctrines, Fosdick developed an approach that marshaled the best learning of his day, pedagogically and psychologically, to reconnect with congregations. And it worked. People had stopped listening, really listening, to sermons, and when Fosdick preached, people heard him, really heard him, heard him by the tens of thousands, and heard him gladly. (One theological critic of Fosdick famously observed, "That man says what I don't believe better than anybody I know.")

Moreover, one wonders if Fosdick himself rigorously followed the method he advocated in *Harper's*. Fosdick says that sermons should address the questions and concerns people bring to church, but one of his gifts was clearly the ability to get people concerned about matters not at all in their heads when they stepped off the subway. Are we really to imagine, for example, that as the congregation of New York's First Presbyterian Church gathered for worship on that spring morning in May of 1922 they entered the sanctuary with the question burning on their lips, "Shall the fundamentalists win?" That, of course, was what Fosdick preached about that day, in what is surely his most famous sermon. In short, Fosdick set the agenda that day and gathered the hearers, indeed, a whole generation of hearers, around him. In other words, like many other great preachers, Fosdick was fortunately not always a follower of his own homiletical advice.

It may be, though, that a generation of preachers took Fosdick's counsel more seriously than he did himself. Distilled to its essence, Fosdick's answer to the question "What is the matter with preaching?" comes down to one main beef: most sermons were not organized around people's needs. On that score, at least, I think we can relax. Fosdick and those who followed him won that battle. Say what you will about the problems of preaching today, you cannot fault most sermons for straying from "people's needs." Most preachers are faithful, if not always artful, practitioners of need-based preaching, and as Fred Craddock once noted, if they cannot quickly identify some human pain to address, they circle like vultures waiting for someone to go down. For the most part, the kind of sermons that caused Fosdick distress, the old bombastic biblical sermons with their clouds of exegetical detail and windy explanations, and the classic thematic sermons with their detailed and thoughtful analyses of some significant topic, exist now only in homiletical Jurassic Parks. Those of us who teach preaching may have our pedagogical shortcomings, but we have been resoundingly successful over the last three-quarters of a century in getting Fosdick's main point across: sermons should connect to the real-life concerns of the hearers and not drift off into abstractions. The problem is, the price we have paid for life-situation preaching has been high.

What's the News?

All of this seems to set us up for an obvious point, namely, that the pendulum needs to swing the other way and that sermons should seek to recover a healthy dose of the very things Fosdick found objectionable. Isn't it true that the homiletical arc courses back and forth between content and context and, while Fosdick was right in his day to advocate for listener-oriented, contextually sensitive sermons, the time has now come, after more than seventy-five years of saturation with context, for the restoration of some biblical and theological content? There are some signs that homiletics as a discipline is beginning to tilt precisely in this direction. For example, the recent appearance of several books on preaching and the Pauline literature presents some evidence of a field grown weary of induction without information, story without substance, therapy without theology. Fosdick's famous quip about biblical preachers was, "Only the preacher . . . [thinks folk] come to church desperately anxious to discover what happened to the Jebusites." A contemporary critic of preaching might well respond that the problem today is that decades of content-thin preaching have left congregations without enough biblical knowledge even to catch Fosdick's little joke.

However, as logical as it may appear, a transfusion of Bible and theology injected directly into the veins of the sermon is not the solution. Indeed, to present the question as one of content versus context is close, but no cigar. In the end, I agree with many of those who say that preaching today is malnourished biblically, theologically, and didactically, but the real dilemma, I would argue, lies elsewhere. Getting right to the point: the main problem with much of today's preaching is that it is simply not newsworthy. By this, I don't mean that preaching is not exciting enough to be covered on CNN. Rather, I mean that what is often lacking from our proclamation of the "good news" is a deep sense of the gospel itself as "news."

In the broadest sense, I am using "news" in the same way the front-page editor of a newspaper would, namely, as an event unusual enough to stand out from the routine and important enough to make a difference in the way people live. In one of his essays, novelist Walker Percy imagines a scientist reading a paper to a convention of other scientists. The paper is filled with data and claims, but in the middle of the presentation the alarm goes out that the convention hall is on fire. Immediately, the scientist reading the paper leans into the microphone and shouts, "Follow me, I know the way out!" Everyone in the hall, claims Percy, can tell the difference between the learned paper and the fire alarm, between the scientific claims and the more urgent claim, "Follow me, I know the way out."[1] The first is information; the second is *news*.

More particularly, I am employing "news" in the theological sense. The "news" that concerns preaching is about something that God has done, is doing, or will do that stands out from the routine events of life and makes a potentially life-changing difference. All Christian preaching is a reverberation of the Easter kerygma, which is of course the "news" par excellence, that Jesus "died. . . , was buried, and . . . was raised on the third day in accordance with the scriptures" (1 Cor. 15:3–4).

If the preaching of the "good news" is not "news," then it cannot qualify as "good." When it comes to Christian proclamation, no news is bad news. Now in his own way Fosdick was onto part of this. What bothered him most about the sermons of his contemporaries was that people didn't care about them, that they made little difference in the real lives of the people who heard them, that they weren't, in this sense, newsworthy. However, what is muted in Fosdick's method (though not always in his practice) is the other side of the definition of "good news," namely, the eventfulness of God's action in life. In Fosdick's essay, the Christian gospel operates more like a philosophy or a set of principles. It has few moving parts, and nothing much is happening in it since it is a static body of knowledge and values. So the real interest and action in preaching is in using this gospel to solve the personal problems of the hearers. But, at its core, the gospel is not a tool placed in the preacher's hands to be used to fix whatever problems and solve whatever puzzles people bring to church. The gospel is news placed in the preacher's mouth. Ever since the women ran back slack-jawed from the empty tomb, the gospel message has been, "News, news! Something happened out there, and life can never be the same."

In *Preaching Paul*, Daniel Patte's fascinating analysis of the preaching of Paul, Patte points to the newsworthy quality of the gospel as Paul proclaimed it. According to Patte, Paul faced a difficult decision in his missionary preaching. He wanted to proclaim the gospel, which he understood primarily in Jewish apocalyptic terms, to a culture molded by Hellenistic thought forms. What should he do? Should he insist that his hearers learn a new vocabulary and adopt Jewish apocalyptic categories? Or should he translate the gospel into Hellenistic formulas? He did neither. Instead he used his Jewish apocalyptic gospel of cross and resurrection as a lens through which to view Hellenistic culture. When he examined the culture of his hearers through this gospel lens, he was able to perceive cross-resurrection events in their culture, that is, places where God could be seen to be active. He began his preaching by pointing to these, by announcing the divine activity in their own lives.[2] "News! News!" Paul announced. "Something is happening out there. God is at work in your world, and life can never be the same."

Listening to Ourselves

Surprising as it may seem, it is precisely this sense of divine eventfulness—that God is at work—that is lacking in much current preaching. This deficiency is not immediately apparent, however, since most sermons are still fully stocked with religious language, calls for spiritual growth, and plentiful reassurances that God loves us, and so forth. In short, many sermons today have plenty of God talk, but precious little news. In *The Church in the Power of the Spirit*, theologian Jürgen Moltmann pictured the liturgical action of preaching this way: "[O]ne person or more gets up in front of the congregation to preach the Gospel. . . . These people come from the community, but come forward in front of it and act in Christ's name."[3] Notice that there are two actions here: the preacher comes *from* the assembly but then stands *in front* of it to act in the name of Christ. Both actions, claims Moltmann, are important. The preacher must come from the congregation if the preaching is to be in the language of the people and address their needs and concerns. This is, of course, Fosdick's point. But the second action is equally important. The preacher must stand in front of the assembly and speak a word that transcends the community, a word spoken in the name of Christ. "After all," said Moltmann, "the . . . community does not want to listen to itself and project its own image of itself."[4]

But this is exactly the problem with much preaching today. It is the community listening to itself and projecting its own image. It has all the requisite Christian vocabulary, but there is nothing newsworthy, no startled announcement of what God is doing. Like a well-played chess game, sermons today can be beautifully constructed and quite well executed, but one gets the sense that they are the product of pieces already on the board and movements already self-contained in the rules and processes at hand. At no point does one get disturbed by a startled cry that the "something" has happened, the tomb is empty, and the world is now changed.

The physicist Niels Bohr once said that he traced his interest in theoretical physics to the childhood experience of gazing into the fishpond at his family home. He would lie down beside the pond for hours, watching the fish. It occurred to him one day that the fish did not know that they were being watched. In fact, the fish were unaware of any reality beyond the confines of the pond. Sunlight streaming in from the outside was, to the fish, simply the inner illumination of the pond. Even when it rained on the pond, as far as the fish were concerned the ripples and splashes were merely events internal to their environment. Bohr wondered if humans were like the fish in this regard, being acted on in multiple dimensions of reality but aware of only one dimension and interpreting all events in their single frame of reference.

Likewise, many sermons are rich in references to God, but a close analysis reveals that what is actually meant by "God" is merely a projection of religious sentiment, something already present and self-contained in the consciousness of the hearers. Take, for example, the following excerpt from a sermon:

> Unresolved grief is the greatest weight on the Christian life. We get stuck somewhere in the stages of grief and cannot move through to acceptance of the facts of death and finally to peace. Jesus said in the Sermon on the Mount, "Blessed are those who mourn," as if to say, "Congratulations to those who can grieve and work through their sadness, work through the anger, work through the loss. These are the blessed ones who can find God's true acceptance and peace."

Now, as sermon talk goes, this seems on the surface to be perfectly acceptable. It alludes to the Bible, refers to God, and constitutes what may well be very wise pastoral counsel about grief. Indeed, many hearers would undoubtedly find these words quite helpful. They would probably recognize, to quote Fosdick again, "that the preacher is tackling something of vital concern to them." They can, as Fosdick urged, "see that [the preacher] is engaged in a serious and practical endeavor to state fairly a problem which actually exists in their lives and then to throw what light on it he can."

So what's the problem? Well, frankly, this isn't news. Mindful of the fact that this paragraph may be but a single facet in a jewel-like sermon with many virtues, nevertheless I would submit that, insofar as this excerpt is representative of the whole sermon, nothing newsworthy occurs in it. At the risk of being too harsh, but to make the point, the preacher here has marched Jesus and the Beatitudes in at sword point to support conventional psychotherapeutic counsel about "good grief." Whether this counsel is healthy or not is beside the point. The point is that it was already fully present in the current cultural competence, and the function of this portion of the sermon is simply to remind us of what our culture already knows to be true and wise and to exhort us to put it into practice.

I don't want to be misunderstood. I am quite aware that a sermon is a complex literary genre, and preaching must press itself to more than one task. Sermons exhort, give sage advice, urge people to do and think a whole host of things. They properly draw insights from many sources, not just the Scripture. A preacher doesn't spend twenty minutes shouting, "The tomb is empty. He is risen!" Eventually someone will respond, "So what?" and that question, and thousand others growing from it, must be addressed. But finally, Christian preaching can claim to be gospel proclamation only if everything that is said rests on the Easter cry, "Something has happened! God has done something, is doing something, will do something world-shaking in our midst." The good news is, after all, *news*.

Luther was, I think, making the same point when he challenged the tendency in his day to preach Christ as an example, as a kind of Moses, "as if Christ did nothing more than teach and provide examples as the other saints do, as if the gospel were simply a textbook of teachings or laws." While acknowledging that the New Testament does, on occasion, present Jesus as an example, Luther claimed that "this is the smallest part of the gospel." What constitutes the essential gospel, Luther said, was not our following of Christ's example but Christ's coming to us as a gift:

> When you open the book containing the Gospels and read or hear how Christ comes here or there, or how someone is brought to him, you should therein perceive the sermon or the gospel through which he is coming to you, or you are being brought to him. *For the preaching of the Gospel is nothing else than Christ coming to us, or we being brought to him.* When you see how he works, however, and how he helps everyone to whom he comes or who is brought to him, *then rest assured that faith is accomplishing this in you* and that he is offering your soul exactly the same sort of help and favor through the gospel. If you pause here and let him do you good, that is, if you believe that he benefits and helps you, then you really have it. Then Christ is yours, presented to you as a gift.[5]

Put sermons, then, to this test: Is there any announcement that God-in-Christ is coming to us and that we are being brought to him? Is there any proclamation that what we see God doing in Scripture is being accomplished even now in us? In sum, does the sermon have any real "news"?

And Now, the News

The Gospel of Mark portrays the ministry of Jesus as beginning with a newsworthy sermon: "Jesus came to Galilee, proclaiming the good news of God, and saying, 'The time is fulfilled, and the kingdom of God has come near; repent, and believe in the good news'" (Mark 1:14–15). Each phrase of Mark's summary of Jesus' message is definitive for what constitutes newsworthy preaching:

1. "*The time is fulfilled*"—Jesus is pointing to the present and saying that something is happening *now*. A measure of gospel preaching is that, even

as it ranges from past to future, there is a present-tenseness about it. Even as it calls on our faithful memories and stimulates future hope, it nevertheless points to what God is doing now, in our presence. The gospel proclamation is always, as Jesus said, "fulfilled in your hearing." Theologian Carl Michalson compared the preacher to the news vendor crying out breaking news in the streets:

> The gospel, which is the good news proclaimed by Christians as something new every day, is at one and the same time the once-for-all news (Rom 6:10, Heb 7:27). It is the *final* edition. One who hears it should have the same sensations once felt when hearing the voice of a newsboy cracking the night with the latest headline on the war, the elections, or the fight.[6]

2. *"The kingdom of God has come near"*—Though one may wish to debate the precise meaning of this phrase, at its core the announcement that "the kingdom of God has come near" says, "Have you heard? God is at work right here in our very neighborhood!" Now that's *news*. The proclamation about the nearness of the kingdom almost surely blends both the temporal and the geographical. In terms of time, the long-expected reign of God is approaching. God has come from the future to the present, and is pounding on the door. Geographically, the activity of God is happening not in some distant heaven or as a perfect idea in a platonic, ideal universe, but down the street, within earshot, even in our own lives. Jesus is the pioneer and perfecter of the role of kingdom courier, announcing the late-breaking news of the nearness of the reign of God.

It is a famous feature of the Gospel of Mark that, at least in the opinion of many scholars, it ends inconclusively. The women who went to the tomb of Jesus on Easter morning are greeted by a young man in a white robe, who tells them that Jesus has been raised, that they are not to be frightened, and that they are to go and tell the disciples that Jesus is going ahead of them to Galilee and the disciples will see him there. Instead, the women flee from the tomb in terror, and—these are the final words of the original manuscript of Mark—"they said nothing to anyone, for they were afraid" (Mark 16:8). That's it. No joyful reunions between the disciples and Jesus, no forward-looking speeches about the mission of the church, no postresurrection appearances. Just frightened women scampering away as fast as their feet will carry them, fear, and silence.

However, the final, broken sentence of Mark's Gospel has the effect on the readers of sending us to Galilee to meet the risen Christ. The Gospel ended on an incomplete note, and somehow we sense that we, the readers, are summoned to close the loop. We are the disciples who are to go to Galilee to meet the risen Christ, who has gone ahead of us. We do not, of course, get on a plane to Israel. Rather we travel to a reader's Galilee, to Mark's Galilee, that is, we turn the pages back and start reading the Gospel again. "Jesus came to Galilee," we read in Mark 1:14, and we read Mark's Gospel once more, this time having been to the cross and to the tomb. This time, though, the stories of Jesus' healing, teaching, casting out demons, confronting the religious authorities, and faithfully following the will of God are not stories of Jesus of Nazareth but of the risen Christ. Taken this way, the whole Gospel of Mark is a series of postresurrection stories. Healing, teaching, casting out demons, confronting the powers, and following God's will are precisely what Christ is doing right now and in our very neighborhood. It is the task of preaching, not simply to tell stories about Jesus, but to look through those stories to discern how they are happening at our doorstep.

At its deepest theological level, then, Christian preaching is concerned with postresurrection appearances of the risen Christ, not in the sense of the apparitions and visitations of the popular mind or the movies, but in the sense that the risen Christ is alive and at work in the world. Faithful preaching is alert to Christ's presence and ready to bear witness to it. Consider, for example, this excerpt from a sermonic essay by Fleming Rutledge. She is talking about the biblical idea of "the wrath of God" as the action of God against all that is evil, and she points to the ministry of Desmond Tutu, who would become bishop, as a place where this action of God is happening now:

> I have a newspaper clipping in my file that dates back to the apartheid era in South Africa. Desmond Tutu, then Anglican bishop of Johannesburg, had just returned from one of his trips abroad where he openly sought support for the fight against the racial policies of his country. At an airport news conference in Johannesburg, he declared that he was not at all worried about his passport being confiscated yet again. Having one's passport taken away is not the worst thing that can happen to a Christian, he said. Even being killed is not the worst thing. "For me, one of the worst things would be if I woke up one day and said to people, 'I think apartheid is not so bad.' For me, this would be worse than death."
>
> This is surely a clue to understanding the wrath of God. A god who remained silent in the face of atrocities would not be the God of

Abraham, Isaac and Jacob or the God and Father of our Lord Jesus Christ. It has been given to Bishop Tutu more than almost anyone else in our time to be the human voice and face of the God who has not remained silent.[7]

What is significant here is that the preacher is not content merely to define the concept of the wrath of God or to narrate places in the Bible where it can be seen. She believes that God is exercising divine wrath here and now in forms such as the work of Desmond Tutu, and she announces this as a present event. She is delivering the *news*.

3. "*Repent, and believe in the good news*"—The idea of repentance has been domesticated and sentimentalized into something akin to feeling sorry for things we have done. In Jesus' proclamation, though, repentance is more like a change of citizenship. Jesus' announcement that the kingdom was at hand is, in essence, news that a revolution has occurred, a new sovereignty has overthrown the current regime, and time has come to switch loyalties. No longer should people obey the laws and customs of the old order, but they should "believe in the good news" of this change in powers and show that they do by living the laws and customs of the new order.

Almost every Christian sermon will contain ethical elements, calls to live in a different way. When a sermon is not newsworthy, however, these ethical exhortations are but appeals to something already at hand in the hearers' moral character. They base their authority on people's guilt or intrinsic goodness. A newsworthy sermon operates out of a quite different moral frame, saying, "Something has happened in our midst. God is acting to set us free, and we do not have to live the old way anymore." In other words, it is the gospel *news* of the gospel that makes the gospel *life* possible.

Conclusion

Jokes abound about boredom in church and people sleeping through sermons. Sadly, under all the humor, there is truth. It is not so much that people actually slumber as we preach; very few do. Rather, people doze with their eyes open, not expecting much because there is often so little newsworthy about what we say. In gospel preaching, no news is bad news. It is encouraging and instructive, I think, to recall the experience many of us who preach have at the beginning of sermons. After the lessons have been read, we stand up to preach, and for fifteen seconds, a beautiful and urgent season, the room is filled with expectation. Yes, many weeks we will soon lose them, lose them to distractions, lose them to their own thoughts, lose them, perhaps, to boredom. But for fifteen seconds, there is breathless anticipation. It is almost as if they are disciples for whom the world has sagged under the weight of living out its days with no good news to give it life. Suddenly there we are at the door, out of breath from our running, faces flush from what we have seen and heard at the empty tomb, and the congregation looks at us with wonderment and expectation, their faces asking, "Is there any news?"

Notes

1. Walker Percy, *The Message in the Bottle: How Queer Man Is, How Queer Language Is, and What One Has to Do with the Other* (New York: Picador, 2000), 138.
2. Daniel Patte, *Preaching Paul* (Philadelphia: Fortress, 1984).
3. Jürgen Moltmann, *The Church in the Power of the Spirit: A Contribution to Messianic Ecclesiology* (New York: Harper and Row, 1977), 303.
4. Ibid.
5. Martin Luther, "Proclamation versus Moralism," in Richard Lischer, ed., *The Company of Preachers: Wisdom on Preaching, Augustine to the Present* (Grand Rapids: Eerdmans, 2002), 118. Italics added.
6. Carl Michalson, "On the Gospel," in Lischer, *Company of Preachers*, 43.
7. Fleming Rutledge, "Coverups (Psalm 85)," *Christian Century*, November 17–24, 1999, 117.

Chapter Ten

What Progress !?

Eugene L. Lowry

R eading the Fosdick article once again in preparation for the writing of this essay has been a peculiar event for me. In many respects the writing feels utterly foreign to our time and place in history. The fact that a secular publisher would even be interested in what one preacher thinks are the current problems of preaching is itself astounding. Given the present place of organized religion in American life, what secular editor today would care? Indeed, the cultural landscape of North America has shifted radically. Likewise, linguistic political correctness without some serious sense of historical location could have open season on Fosdick's recurring emphasis on such terms as "experience," "problem solving," and "human needs."

The devotees of George Lindbeck's categorizations would have a field day, perhaps overlooking the interface of the personal and the corporate in Fosdick's work. He could easily be scorned for the sin of "experiential-expressivist" heresy, and dismissed for rank subjectivism— but only by those who have not, for example, heard or read his prophetic blockbuster sermon of November 21, 1943: "Worshiping the Gods of a Beaten Enemy."[1] There he was, in the middle of the Second World War, preaching from the pulpit of "the cathedral of North American Protestantism," Riverside Church, New York, and citing Nietzsche's line "When you fight a monster, beware lest you become a monster."[2] This sermon on racism by the pacifist preacher at "John D. Rockefeller's church" hardly qualifies him as subjectivist psychologizer. Yet his language use often is difficult to grasp adequately and fairly, given our changing linguistic idioms. Likewise, Fosdick's emphasis on human experience would have to dodge the slings and arrows of the more radical sort of postliberals.

Indeed, Enlightenment assumptions about the possibilities for public arenas for conversation would have to be renegotiated.

Nevertheless, in terms of some central homiletic challenges we face today, the article seems exactly on target for the opening years of the new millennium. Certainly, his central concern for method and shape—and behind that, the questions of divine revelation and hence purpose of preaching—should be our central concerns still. His assessment of the different worlds of preacher talk and people-on-the-street think is an earlier way to name our current concerns about language and practices.

Utilizing an adaptation of the four sermon analytic categories named by Lucy Rose in *Sharing the Word*, I propose to name what I believe to be several aspects of homiletics that appear to fit the question, "What is the matter with preaching today?"[3] In particular, our approach will be to ask what may be amiss today relative to sermonic *shape*, *purpose*, *content*, and *language*. Actually, these four categories do not and cannot really refer to separable entities. Such a division would constitute an awkward and arbitrary format. Given the close interrelationship of these four foci, it will be better to think of them as four interfacing homiletical variables.

Shape

Perhaps the major theme raised by Fosdick in the *Harper's Magazine* article, and clearly the one woven throughout the writing was the issue of sermonic shape. "The fault generally lies, not in the essential quality of the [preacher's] mind or character, but in . . . mistaken methods," Fosdick concluded. At one perhaps overgenerous moment he described the all-too-common sermon: "The text was good and the truth was undeniable. The subject was well chosen and well developed but, for all that, nothing happened. . . . The reason for this can commonly be traced to one cause: the preacher started [the] sermon at the wrong end." Well, what a coincidence! This central issue has not changed in the span of more than seventy-five years.

Fosdick meant "wrong end" in several different ways. The first sense had to do with the tendency of "thinking first of [one's own] ideas, original or acquired," instead of thinking "first of [the] people." The issue here is "organizing [the] sermon around the elucidation of [a] theme," rather than beginning at the point of some important concern pressing in upon the congregation's lives.

The second sense of "wrong end" was that "instead of starting with a text, they start with their own ideas on some subject of their choice." As a result, says Fosdick, "Week after week one sees these topical preachers who turn their pulpits into platforms and the sermons into lectures."

Now, all these years later, we may discover on the back page of the Sunday bulletin an incomplete ("please fill in the blank") outline of the lecture. Our task is to stay awake long enough to catch the pithy line that will fit exactly into the blank at point I. A. (2). We need not worry about missing the next several sentences of the sermon as preached while writing in the right phrase; the preacher will not have strayed forward very far. Can you imagine a humorist cuing the audience about a sidesplitting joke about to happen with the admonition: "Please take notes, the punch line is close!"?

Fosdick's complaint was not limited to those topical preachers who began with an idea rather than a congregational issue. The third sense of "starting at the wrong end," he said, is committed by expository preachers who ignore the people in favor of a text. He described their faulty process:

> They take a passage from Scripture and, proceeding on the assumption that the people attending church that morning are deeply concerned about what the passage means, they spend their half hour or more on historical exposition of the verse or chapter, ending with some appended practical application to the auditors. Could any procedure be more surely predestined to dullness and futility? . . . Nobody else who talks to the public so assumes that the vital interests of the people are located in the meaning of words spoken two thousand years ago.

Were Fosdick writing the article today, no doubt he would speak of the failure of the preacher to notice the remarkable gap of social location between pulpit and pew.

My way of describing this continuing problem—whether born of topical or expository preaching—is in the fact of beginning with an answer and then unpacking it by means of deductive processes. Craddock rightly noted that all honest exegesis is inductive in form, not deductive. Said he: "If exegesis has to labor under the burden of providing particular support for a dogmatic conclusion already occupying one's mind, it ceases to be exegesis."[4] Moreover, as I noted in *The Homiletical Plot*, "It is imperative that the preacher not discard the struggle of the study and simply report the results in the pulpit."[5] "It bears repeating," Craddock concluded, "that a preaching event is a sharing in the Word, a trip not just a destination, an arriving at a point for drawing conclusions. . . . It is unnatural and unsatisfying to be in a place to which you have not traveled."[6] In short, I believe every sermon—whether preached in 1928 or in 2004—ought to move from opening disequilibrium of some type, through complication and decisive turn, toward resolution born of the gospel. Indeed, given the changing state of technology and communication in the world in which we now live, all this is even more crucial than before. What is at stake here, as Craddock so crisply put it elsewhere, "is not to get something said but to get something heard."[7] So, what does it take to maximize the chance of getting something heard?

Quite a number of years ago, I experienced great pain in my right wrist, making holding a briefcase or turning a key a nearly impossible task. The specialist's questions of me began moving toward an obvious fork in the diagnostic road. Was this a case of carpal tunnel syndrome, or the onset of arthritis? Based on the examination, the doctor was unsure. "We'll have to wait until your condition gets worse to see," he said, "because by then some of the symptoms will lessen and some increase, and hence diagnostic clarity will be possible." Meanwhile, the matter prompted a dilemma: Should I follow the advice to suspend the wrist in case I am suffering from carpal tunnel syndrome, or should I keep the wrist in constant motion in case this is the onset of arthritis? How about a sling for the morning suspension and constant rotation for the afternoon? To do nothing in particular seemed the best compromise. As it turned out, the pain simply went away.

I related this story to a group of pastors in Chicago some time later—attempting to undergird the notion that exploration of the sermonic issue requires complication in order to press the matter toward clarity born of the gospel. During the break, a nurse-turned-clergy enlightened me—naming exactly my symptoms, and revealing that my pain was caused by neither of the two options that had been considered, but a third option instead. Unfortunately, I have been unable to remember the proper diagnosis the nurse so wisely gave. Clearly it was the truth. Why can I never recall it? Because, in Chicago, the pain was already gone; the presenting issue was absent. When sermons begin with answers, they become resolutions without issues, truths without experiential context. Not only are they not memorable; they are utterly empty. To shape sermons this way is to start at the wrong end, just as Fosdick reported in 1928. Without something at stake in the sermon process, the congregation can scarcely hear the preacher, let alone receive the transforming Word.

Yet, this issue of sermonic shape—of moving from issue to resolution—is not reducible simply to a flat kind of problem-solution mentality. The "itch," as in itch-to-scratch methodology first must be transformed into an issue of profound importance. The worst-case abuse of issue-resolution sermonic shape occurs when the preacher defines the issue superficially, avoids any in-depth escalation of the matter, and thus triumphantly announces the "resolution." Often, such treatment turns into some form of ethic of obedience: "Have faith . . . do better . . ." (or even worse: "Do better and then find faith").

Fosdick was quite aware of all this when he said, "The danger involved in starting a sermon with a problem is that the very word *problem* suggests something to be merely debated and its solution may suggest nothing more than the presentation of a helpful idea to the mind." Sometimes, he observed, preachers "had been so anxious to deal with felt needs in the congregation that they forgot to arouse the consciousness of need unfelt but real." Such preaching, he observed, moves to the "practically trivial," and indeed, "narrowed to the conscious needs of mediocre people." Such "perversions," said Fosdick, "would wreck any method whatsoever."

Purpose

I believe we may be moving toward a crisis in North American preaching regarding the question of homiletical purpose—an issue of perhaps even greater proportion than at the time of Fosdick's writing. Part of the problem, but only part, is that we are in the midst of a major historical transition. We are between the times. This transition is from a print-based culture inaugurated in the sixteenth century with the invention of the printing press with movable type, to the now-emerging electronic culture, dominated by the screen. At stake in this crisis, I believe, is a growing reduction of proclamation to that of instruction.

Although instruction often is a part of proclamation, by itself it stops short of preaching's aim. As we have already noted, Fosdick was very clear about how idea-based sermons easily degenerate into lectures. But the "real sermon must do more than discuss joy," he declared; "it must produce it." He then moves on to name "a basic distinction between a sermon and an essay." Note his bottom-line expectation when he complains that

> the outstanding criticism popularly and properly launched against a great deal of our modern, liberal preaching is that though it consists of neat, analytical discourses, pertinent to real problems and often well conceived and well phrased, it does nothing to anybody. Such sermons are not sermons but essays. It is lamentably easy to preach feebly about repentance without making anybody feel like repenting, or to deliver an accomplished discourse on peace without producing

> any of that valuable article in the auditors. . . . [The] true preacher
> . . . does more than discuss a subject; [the preacher] produces the
> thing itself in the people who hear it.

Here, he sounds a lot like Henry Mitchell, who insists that every sermon must have a "behavioral purpose," which he believes to be "second only to the scriptural text" in importance.[8]

Unfortunately, says Fosdick, the lecturers "are keyed to argumentation rather than creation. They produce essays, which means that they are chiefly concerned with the elucidation of a theme." But the sermon, he says, is about "transformation."

Now, of course, differing preaching traditions have differing definitions of the homiletical aim. While the traditional preacher sees preaching as a matter of *transmission*—an "engineering operation," says Fosdick, "by which a chasm is spanned"—kerygmatic preachers (to follow Rose's categories) are more likely to view preaching as *announcement* mediated by the preacher. Those of us in what is sometimes called "the New Homiletic" are more likely to view the purpose of preaching as *evocation*. As James Cone puts it: "The Word is more than *words* about God. God's Word is a poetic happening, an evocation of an indescribable reality in the lives of the people."[9]

Whatever the tradition, preaching is intended as revelatory event. This is utterly different from explanation or elucidation or elaboration—or even exposition. One way or another, preaching is intended as a corporate experience in the congregation. As David Buttrick rightly claims: "Preaching constructs in consciousness a 'faith-world' related to God."[10]

One particularly significant factor in contemporary North American church life that has, I believe, inadvertently contributed to this reduction from proclamation to instruction is the widespread use of the three-year lectionary. Frankly, while expecting it to be accepted fully by those within Roman Catholic, Episcopalian, and Lutheran judicatories, I have been surprised at the enormously growing use of the lectionary for preaching in United Methodist, Disciples, Presbyterian, and Baptist congregations as well. For many of us, it has become a new biblical day in our history. And often it has increased the unity and organic flow of worship.

Yet, in spite of all this, including the increasing availability of resources for significant liturgical opportunities that lectionary use provides, two significantly major concerns often arise in the use of the lectionary for preaching. First, the lectionary selection committee delights in summary resolution texts, while often avoiding any issues that might be raised by the text. (This is based partly on what is called the "doxological purpose" involved in lectionary selections.) As a result, it can be difficult to make the potentially powerful homiletical move from presenting issue to final resolution when no presenting issue has been provided by the text selected. Moreover, it is worth noticing that it is not unusual for several "troubling" verses of a pericope to have been omitted, so that no one will be bothered by an issue.

Second, in some circles a dangerous trend is now occurring in the use of the manifold lectionary resources available—books, journals, and Internet connections. These various resources range greatly in quality, of course. Some are wonderful; some are not. Yet, even with the best resources, often an instructional modality accompanies them. After these resources provide explanatory meaning of the text for those of us who preach, now we are able to explain to the congregation what the text is all about. The unfortunate resulting genre of meaning that is established provides but a very short and tempting distance between preaching and instructing. As Fosdick has reminded us, preaching is not "elucidation of a theme," and the sermon is not an essay. Clearly, the pulpit must not become a lectern in the lecture hall.

Content

Closely related to the question of homiletical shape and purpose is the issue of sermonic content. There is, of course, great variety in sermonic content because there is great diversity of theological and denominational traditions, to say nothing of the significant diversity of occasions. Yet a strange phenomenon has entered the liturgical scene that seems to transcend the varieties of tradition, theology, and occasion. This phenomenon is the growing amount of "user-friendly" experiences sometimes called "contemporary worship."

Before exploring the dangers of what I term a form of homiletical abuse, I want to be clear about the need for liturgical innovation. Just as the lectionary has brought the Bible back to the gathered church for many people, even helping to launch long-term Bible-study courses, so liturgical innovation is now required to keep the church from becoming a museum piece.

As surely as Fosdick was concerned to connect with real people and the diverse issues that people actually face, personally and corporately, so we need a firm commitment to "pitch tent" with the younger generations we are barely reaching. Objection to reaching out to nonprint people with the gospel by means of nonprint media is often little more than a defensive form of arrogance. The invention of the printing press with movable type changed the face of Christianity in the sixteenth century; no less a radical change will transpire in the first half of the twenty-first century, given the radical technological changes now occurring.

At the same time, we need to notice what has happened in some circles of liturgical innovation. Along with avoiding expressly Christian visual symbols in some megachurch parking lots, and symbol avoidance in worship settings, now worship in certain quarters has turned into a kind of "me and Jesus feel good" experience. (Sometimes even Jesus gets left out.) Moreover, in such environs the sermon often is not much more than a few helpful hints about how to still feel good on Tuesday.

It is helpful to recall Fosdick's warning about preaching reduced to "nothing more than the presentation of a helpful idea to the mind." More pointedly, he was concerned about preachers who do not consider people's "mistaken ideas of joy" as well as their "false attempts to get it."

I recall attending a service in a megachurch the very first Sunday after the Columbine tragedy in Littleton, Colorado. Unfortunately, the chosen theme for the day was *teddy bears*, positioned all over the stage, pictured on the bulletin cover, duly considered by liturgical leaders, and named as appropriate objects for deep appreciation by all of us present. But these cute little teddy bears apparently could not be displaced for congregational wrestling with a national tragedy born of despair, sin, and death. Self-affirmation was the key for the day, not the power of the gospel.

It is interesting that often in such services even the term "sermon" is avoided. Terms like "lesson," or "message" are preferred. Part of me is glad the title "sermon" is not used. Whatever minor helpful hints these are, indeed sermons they are not.

It is noteworthy just how these little helpful thoughts are formed. Although film clips may be used to "enliven" the message, the actual shape of the thoughts presented reveals a style of communication seldom taught anymore in preaching classes (or even Speech 101 in college). Moreover, being asked to fill in an incomplete outline form in the back of the bulletin suggests that the message has been pushed far from the oral/aural modality appropriate for the preaching event.

Language

In Lucy Rose's book, the differing forms of preaching naturally result in differing language modalities. For example, sermonic *announcement* as *witness* by the "kerygmatic" preacher is never intended to be as strategic as the *persuasive techniques* of traditional preaching, because of differing understandings about the aims of preaching. Likewise, language geared toward *evocation*, as "New Homiletic" preachers would want, is quite different from the *open-ended* language suitable for conversational preaching, as Rose understands these options. Every preacher's practice of preaching will of course reveal a wide span of language use—depending on text, theme, purpose, and occasion. Yet the ultimate reference point for preaching, regardless of form, has to do with the nature of the gospel itself. And homiletical clarity, which is sought by all, must never defile the Mystery. Warning against "direct frontal speech," Walter Brueggemann declares, "The act of sacrament requires the speech of poetry to keep hidden what must not be profaned by description."[11] Here he is not referring to the possible inclusion of some poem within a sermon; he is describing the character of homiletic address itself.

Indeed, I have noticed that as long as one is talking about matters not very important, words tend to work quite well. But the deeper the subject matter, the greater the claim of the theme, the more words seem to slip away from meaningful adequacy. As R. E. C. Browne put it: "Poets . . . never mean exactly what they say because they cannot say exactly what they mean."[12] With wonderful clarity, the Dutch theologian Hendrikus Berkhof notes that the first thing God reveals about God's self is God's hiddenness, something that we might have surmised even before. As a result, observes Berkhof: "Revelation initiates us into a great mystery." Indeed, "The more we come to know [God] . . . the less we are able to comprehend [God] . . . with our intellect."[13] Sallie McFague TeSelle reminds us that "poetry does not illustrate meaning, it creates it," and hence the church always needs "metaphoric tease"—"through seeing similarity in dissimilars"—when attempting to speak about God.[14] R. E. C. Browne concludes that our preaching must of necessity be content finally with "gestures," because "the ineffable remains the ineffable."[15] No wonder Browne, himself a poet as well as preacher, spoke of the commonality of the work of the poet and that of the preacher. Then along comes Brueggemann with the powerful work aptly titled *Finally Comes the Poet*—a book about preaching.

But mystery, metaphor, and the poet's gesture seem increasingly rare in the pulpit these days. Instead, sermonic language often seems not only to have lost its metaphoric tease into the heart of mystery, but, indeed, to have settled for rather pedestrian informational language more related to minor repair or mechanical adjustment in life, a kind of means-end rationality process. I recall several occasions recently when a very curious image has been utilized by laypersons in response to the ordinary language found in such Sunday services. Sometimes faithful parishioners describe the reasoning behind their continued committed Sunday morning worship attendance as: "Well, I need my batteries recharged every week." Batteries recharged? It is a telling remark.

Some of us are familiar with the automobile amperage gauge. It shows a minus (–) sign on the left and a plus (+) sign on the right. On average, the car's generator needs to maintain at least a middle zero (0) needle mark for the engine to continue running properly. Otherwise, the battery will run down and the car cease functioning. The metaphor suggests the role of the worship service is to prevent spiritual battery rundowns. The idea has a kind of homeostatic presumption, a need not to be drained of spiritual energy. One must get back at least to zero.

Note how this plays itself out in some sermons whose modus operandi appears to be that of countering people's potentially "empty" state of having a dead battery. If there is a need, meet it; if there is confusion, clarify it; if there is a void, fill it; if there is a hurt, heal it—or at least anesthetize it. In short, whatever might be the obstacle, find a way around it. This "satisfaction of a lack" method can take on numerous styles and theological options. What is missing here is any substantive sense of Divine lure, some transcendent claim of the reign of God on human existence that might prompt desire, or what Moltmann named "the passion for life" in a book by the same title.[16]

On the other hand, I remember well a hymn from the days of my youth, a favorite nineteenth-century hymn I first found in the Cokesbury hymnal our congregation was using. Immediately I felt something quite stirring in the congregation's singing of the hymn. It has never lost its grip on me and countless others. Perhaps that is why "Jesus Calls Us" is still included in the latest United Methodist hymnal. From the opening line, "Jesus calls us o'er the tumult . . ." to the closing line of "serve and love thee best of all," it was clear that the gospel operates on a different channel altogether from the world.[17] Sometimes the gospel's call is "above," sometimes "more than," occasionally "in spite of," even perhaps "instead of" this world's lure. I didn't always know for sure what we were supposed to do or be, but always the summons summoned. Indeed, the content of the summons has been multiple in form and diverse in result. Its power stems from the capacity of that hymn to evoke the transcendent and its claims.

The language of preaching must never be reduced to petty problem solving or lectionary explanation or topical edification, the kind of bland preaching Fosdick called "practically trivial." Preaching's purpose is to evoke the mystery of the gospel. Hence, the role of pulpit language is to gesture toward that "God of grace and God of glory" who can "crown thine ancient church's story," who can "free our hearts to work and praise," who should "shame our wanton, selfish gladness," and finally move us toward "serving thee whom we adore."[18]

Notes

1. Harry Emerson Fosdick, *A Great Time to Be Alive* (New York: Pocket Books, 1954), 139–46.
2. Ibid., 141.
3. Lucy Atkinson Rose, *Sharing the Word* (Louisville, Ky.: Westminster John Knox, 1997).
4. Fred B. Craddock, *As One Without Authority* (Enid, Okla.: Phillips University, 1971), 124. This volume has been republished by Chalice Press more recently (2001), under the same title.
5. Eugene L. Lowry, *The Homiletical Plot* (Atlanta: John Knox, 1980), 84. This volume has also been republished recently (2001) by Westminster John Knox, in an expanded edition.
6. Craddock, *As One Without Authority*, 146.
7. Fred B. Craddock, *Preaching* (Nashville: Abingdon, 1985), 167.
8. Henry H. Mitchell, *Celebration and Experience in Preaching* (Nashville: Abingdon, 1990), 53.
9. James H. Cone, *God of the Oppressed* (New York: Seabury, 1975), 18.
10. David Buttrick, *Homiletic* (Philadelphia: Fortress, 1987), 456.
11. Walter Brueggemann, *Finally Comes the Poet* (Minneapolis: Fortress, 1989), 27.
12. R. E. C. Browne, *The Ministry of the Word* (Philadelphia: Fortress, 1976), 70.
13. Hendrikus Berkhof, *Christian Faith* (Grand Rapids: Eerdmans, 1979), 53–54.
14. Sallie McFague TeSelle, *Speaking in Parables* (Philadelphia: Fortress, 1975), 104, 49.
15. Browne, *Ministry of the Word*, 27.
16. Jürgen Moltmann, *The Passion for Life* (Philadelphia: Fortress, 1978).
17. Words by Cecil Frances Alexander, in *The United Methodist Hymnal* (Nashville: United Methodist Publishing House, 1989), no. 398.
18. Ibid., no. 577; words by Harry Emerson Fosdick.

Chapter Eleven

The Weekly Wrestling Match

Barbara Brown Taylor

A sking a bunch of preachers what is the matter with preaching is like asking a bunch of opera singers what is the matter with opera. How would we know? All we can tell you is what it takes to rise to this call—to love these words, to believe in this music, to produce these sounds with absurd faith in their power to heal the living and raise the dead—but once they are out of our mouths, we lose all control over them. Our speech falls on ears as different as the faces they frame. What sounds like justice to one sounds like judgment to another. What sounds like pablum to one sounds like God's own manna to another. At the very least, this suggests that gospel truth is less what is said than what is heard, and that those who listen to sermons on a regular basis are the best ones to ask about what is the matter with preaching.

If preachers do not do that very often, then it is because we already know what people are saying—if not about us, then about other preachers—and the criticism is either so painful to hear or so impossible to resolve that we decide to ignore it. What many of us do instead is to attend preaching conferences where we can polish our skills in the presence of fellow preachers. We meet with other local preachers to find out what they are preaching. We subscribe to print or online journals that supply us with stories and sermon ideas from preachers who are considered expert enough to have their stories and ideas published in such places. Then we craft sermons that are variations on their themes, so that we know we are close to the truth, at least, and that anyone who criticizes us is really criticizing the experts instead.

If I were to choose one single thing that is the matter with preaching today, then it would be the way that habits like these encourage both preachers and their listeners to think of the sermon as a solo performance piece that is brought to the congregation from beyond them some-where—from the biblical, theological, and homiletical experts—instead of from the God in their midst who gives them their lives.

The truly great preachers in this world are people whose names no one will ever know, because their sermons both arise from and are entirely absorbed by local communities of listeners who labor with them to embody God's word. In cases such as these, the success of a sermon is not measured by how many people said they liked it, nor by a preacher's own sense of accomplishment, but by how the spoken word cleared a space for people to be met and set in motion by the Spirit of the living God. When that happens, ownership of the sermon shifts from the one to the many.

The "how to" of such a shift takes different forms in different places, but in places I know about it begins with weekly meetings between preachers and selected representatives of the congregation, who gather to read, study, discuss, and pray in the presence of God and one another. They do this in confidence that together they may be able to discern the ways in which the beating pulse of the Scripture before them and the beat-ing pulse of the world in which they live coincide, and because they believe in this coincidence they are rarely disappointed.

Once the connections become clear to them, they form a question or identify an area of concern that they believe is central to the life of the congregation, and then they send the preacher off—equipped with their insights, stories, and blessings—to compose a sermon that addresses the theme they have developed together. In this way, the preacher serves as their representative person, or parson, whose job is not to produce tasty morsels for their consumption but to speak with them and for them in the seeking of God's will.

On this point as well as everything else I want to say, I hereby give up trying to be original. Fosdick was there first, writing more than seventy-five years ago about preaching in ways that still ring true. His language is old-fashioned and his frame of reference exclusively male, but by focus-ing on the preacher's responsibility to address the lived experience of real human beings, he chooses a theme that strikes me as thoroughly post-modern. While he knows that his "project method" can become "nar-rowed to the conscious needs of mediocre people," Fosdick will not give up on passionately dialogical preaching that serves the vital concerns of human living. Those who worry that he does not say enough about God may miss his point. The gospel manifest in his essay is that God too cares passionately about the vital concerns of human living, enough to send one particular Galilean preacher to embody what it means to "[drench] a congregation with one's lifeblood."

It is the last sentence of Fosdick's essay, however, that intrigues me most. That sentence is the one that I will use to frame my own essay. "Preaching," he writes, "is wrestling with individuals over questions of life and death, and until that idea of it commands a preacher's mind and method, eloquence will avail him little and theology not at all." This definition intrigues me on at least three counts. In the first place, it is not a skill-based one. In the second place, it describes a kind of preaching that takes both time and risks. And in the third place, it is more interested in life than in religion.

I

Preachers can get by without eloquence or learning, Fosdick says more than once in his essay (which makes you wonder if he served on the boards of any seminaries). What their congregations need from them is not brilliance, but bravery, as they consent to wrestle in public—and broad daylight—with the same giants that their listeners face alone at night.

Like many of my peers, I come from a generation of preachers that has been encouraged to think of preaching as the regular practice of a range of skills. Competent exegesis, congregational analysis, concrete imagery, and good eye contact are all on the list. So are the selection of a single theme and function for the sermon and the ruthless elimination of any material that does not serve them. Some of my preacher friends learned to fill out worksheets on their sermons while they were in seminary, and others have devised their own systems based on their own preaching styles.

I am one of those preachers who love ancient languages, and I wish I had more skills in that area. Since I am an Episcopalian and not a Presbyterian, I was required to take only one language in seminary, which means that I can look up Hebrew words on my own but I need a lot of help with Greek. My first year out of graduate school I lived on lentils so that I could afford all ten volumes of Kittel's *Theological Dictionary of the New Testament*. To this day I spend a small fortune on books every year, since I am convinced that every verse of the Bible would open up to me like a dinner plate dahlia if I only knew enough about the language and times in which it was written.

Every preacher has his or her own quirks in the areas of preparation and composition, but when it comes to delivery, a preacher's techniques are like a cook's knives. Some of us type our manuscripts in 24-point font with two-inch margins all around so that the words fairly leap up at us from the page. Others devise outlines so ingenious that they look like secret code. I know preachers who practice their gestures so diligently that their hands run through them reflexively as they are drifting off to sleep, and others who work with voice coaches for a variety of reasons.

The problem with all of this, of course, is that our listeners are often so ornery that they do not fully appreciate how truly skillful we are. In a single congregation of less than a hundred members it is possible for a preacher to hear that people love her crafted sermons, think her sermons are too crafted; love her scholarly approach, think her approach is too scholarly; love her humor, think humor has no place in the pulpit; love her gestures, think her gestures are distracting.

Preachers who try to fix this problem by becoming yet more skillful not only set themselves an impossible task; they also perpetuate the illusion that effective sermons are produced by experts with professional degrees instead of by people who are willing to stay up nights wrestling the same demons and angels that their listeners do—both as one of them and on their behalf.

I am not arguing against those who wish to be skillful preachers, especially since I am one of them, but I am arguing that skills alone are not enough. Before a preacher knows how to read biblical texts in their original languages, tell wonderful stories, employ rhetorical strategies, or make full use of vocal range, a preacher needs to know how to be human. This is especially true in light of all the pressure on preachers—from both within and without—to be *more* than human.

While church members try to hide their beer cans from us in the checkout line at the grocery store and act scandalized if they see us at the gym in stretch pants trying to do yoga, they secretly hope that we know what it is like to walk around in bodies that do not always look, act, or feel the way that we want them to; that we are familiar with the full range of human emotions, including rage, lust, and greed; that we too wake up in the middle of the night terrified of dying in spite of everything that we formally believe, and that there are times when every shred of evidence we have collected for the existence of God can seem to us like no more than wishful thinking.

Even if they do not want us to admit to such things very often, they remain vitally invested in our knowing them, because if we do not, then we do not know them, and we cannot wrestle any of the nighttime visitors that they know best. While eloquence and learning are great boons to any preacher, it is the preacher's hands-on experience of the human condition and willingness to speak of it without guile that makes him or her worth listening to at all.

II

Preachers who already know this also know that preaching from life is much harder than preaching from books, and that wrestling nighttime visitors on your congregation's behalf takes a lot more time than downloading illustrations from a Web site. Even when you emerge from the fray, limping and out of breath, with something to say that you believe is true, your own words can sound less lovely or less authoritative than someone else's words, so that you are always tempted to become a dummy on someone else's knee.

But watch your listeners' faces when you stop speaking for yourself and start quoting extensively from someone else. They can usually bear up for a sentence or two, especially when you are widening the circle of the conversation to include kinds of people who do not happen to attend your church or live in your town, but once it seems clear that you are going to yield your privileged place in front of them so that someone they have never met may address them in your stead, then you can almost see them taking themselves away from you, as you are taking yourself away from them. They did not come to hear someone else. They came to hear you. They want the voice that goes with your body, the voice that knows this community better than anyone else. If you are not willing to risk sounding dumb and vulnerable in public, then why should they? If you won't speak to them from your heart about what really matters, then who will?

Of all the complaints I hear about what is the matter with preaching today, the most common is that the preacher seems to have composed the sermon on the way to church. Sometimes this is simply a curt way of dismissing both the speech and the speaker, but other times I know it is true, because even the preacher will admit it. Ask him why and he will tell you that last week was worse than usual, with an unexpected funeral following the unexpected heart attack of the only person who really knew anything about the church's investments—and all of this during graduation week, when the preacher had already agreed to deliver the baccalaureate sermon at the local high school and present gifts to the church's graduating seniors on Sunday. But it was only a little worse than usual, he may go on to admit, since every week holds human crises that no one saved time for, while the machinery of committee meetings, denominational duties, church mailings, and teacher recruitment yields for no woman or man.

For some preachers, driving to church on Sunday morning is often the first free moment that they have had all week, which points not only to the exhausting expectations placed on clergy by their congregations but also to those that clergy place on themselves. I hope that I am not the only parson to practice a stern rebuke in the mirror to all those people out there who want so much from me—who do not seem to have the least bit of respect for my limits—only to realize with my mouth still open that I am delivering the rebuke to the only (or at least the first) person who needs to hear it. It is no small thing, to be called to seek and serve Christ in all persons. It is no small thing, to want to be loved by the same people whom you have been given to love.

The curious truth is that in order to serve them well you must withdraw from them from time to time, and since you are not going to get agreement from any two of them about when that time might be, you will have to decide for yourself, with no one to tell you that you are a good person who is doing the right thing. But if you do *not* do that, then you not only run the risk of growing to resent those whom you meant to serve but you may also starve your soul, and a starved soul produces mighty thin sermons.

Since some preachers are revived by solitude while others thrive on human company, there is no one answer that fits all, but most of us need both in order to plump up our souls and round out our lives. A good rule is to find your comfort level so that you can leave it on a regular basis, spending time with people (although not necessarily church people) when you would rather hole up in your study, and spending time alone when you would rather lose yourself in a crowd. While there are certainly those of us who feed on the depths of others because we are afraid to plumb our own, that is not the best plan. There is no wrestling other people's nighttime visitors until you know your own by name.

Preachers who cannot seem to protect time for sermon preparation are often the same people who are short on time for prayer, rest, and intimate relationships as well, which means that any attempt to change their priorities is likely to constitute a wrestling match of its own. If that turns out to be the case, then all the better, since there is not a single one of our listeners who does not struggle with the same angel. With so little time, really—not only in a day but also in a life—what shall any of us do with this one wild and precious gift?[1]

III

That brings me to my third and final variation on Fosdick's theme, which is that effective preaching is more interested in life than in religion. If our times seem more troubling than most, then that is because they are *our* times and not someone else's times. And yet there really are a few things about our times that make them different from those that have gone before.

Even five years ago, I would have said that Christendom really was over, but I am not so sure about that anymore. While mainline churches may be emptying out all over Europe and North America, there is convincing evidence that the next chapter of Christian history will be written in the southern hemisphere—not by foreign missionaries there, but by indigenous Christians who have already begun sending their own missionaries north to call the Western nations back to God.

Meanwhile, the political rhetoric surrounding the events of September 11, 2001, has been fundamentally religious rhetoric, which for some of us is as troubling when we hear it in the mouths of our own leaders as when we hear it in the mouths of those on the other side. To decide which nations do and do not constitute an "axis of evil" may be helpful for the purposes of launching preemptive strikes, but what happens when the children of immigrants from those same nations are citizens of our own? At my goddaughter's public school graduation from fifth grade in 2002, I clapped for Sofia Bibliowicz, Yasmeen Malik, Wollinsky Mendez, and Erin Yu-Lee, as well as Madeline Jones.

Many of us are no longer able to protect the illusion that the United States is a Christian nation or even a Judeo-Christian nation. It is, instead, the most religiously diverse nation on the face of the earth, where globalization is not something we read about in the *Wall Street Journal* but something we encounter at the grocery store, where exotic-smelling things such as lemon grass and dried tamarind are showing up in the produce section, or on the expressway, where we cannot read the billboards because they are not designed to attract our business but the business of those for whom English is a second language. As long as there are plenty of jobs to go around and the invisible boundaries between different neighborhoods remain intact, peace may prevail, but sometimes that peace is less like a river than like a pool of nitroglycerin. Introduce one spark— one teenage romance across racial lines, one Laotian community petitioning the local zoning board for permission to use an old house for a Buddha hall—and the whole thing can go up with a bang.

While some of us are eager to befriend these new neighbors, the irony of our inclusiveness is not lost on us. As we are busy trying to get to know neighbors of other faiths, our relationships with those of our own faith are more and more fractured. My own denomination, the Episcopal Church, managed to survive the Civil War without breaking in two as some others did, but now we have clergy ordained by Asian and African bishops who are operating independently from those ordained by American bishops, so that our schism is well under way.

Meanwhile, two of the three historical branches of the Christian church continue to practice closed Communion, while Protestants who do not agree on why, how, or when to baptize people continue to argue about who may be ordained. None of these are small matters, but most days I would rather talk with a Buddhist about Buddhism than with a fellow Christian about Christianity, if only because I know that we will have less in common to fight about. I also know what a weak excuse that is for not loving the neighbors who are nearest to me. With this and everything else that I have said in mind, I think that Christian preachers who are still confronting secularism as the greatest threat to faith might do well to check their backsides from time to time, since it seems entirely likely that the next great battles of faith will take place among the faithful.

Many of us will never forget the sermons that we preached or heard on the Sunday after 9/11, not only because the proclamation of the Word had never seemed so important to us before, but also because many of us looked out at congregations larger than any we had seen for quite a while. In most cases, they included at least a few people who had never stepped foot inside a church before, who were there not only because they were frightened and confused, but also because they wanted to know what Christian faith had to say in the face of real terror.

In Fosdick's terms, the presenting problem that day was how a good God could allow such a terrible thing to happen, but right behind that one, I believe, were two more problems that remain fundamental to anyone who still bothers to go to church: (1) What, if anything, makes Christians different from everyone else? and (2) How are Christians called to live with everyone else, including those who may wish them dead?

While other, more domestic questions may be the ones that keep most people up at night, I hope that preachers do not neglect to wrestle these two primary ones as well, both because I have heard some very scary answers to them from high-profile Christians in recent months (*Muhammad was a terrorist?*) and because the peace of the world may well depend on how the citizens of the wealthiest, most powerful nation on earth—which happens also to be one of the most religiously diverse—answer these questions.

Both questions concern the subject of religious identity, which has become so contentious in our times that many people, both young and old, have traded in religion for spirituality. While they take a lot of abuse, especially from religious professionals, the reasons for their defection are often quite honorable. Having noted the ways in which religions divide people from one another, they are seeking a way that unites them instead —a way that tends to focus more on practice than on belief. Whether they are praying, drumming, or meditating together, they are hunting for an experience of the holy that will bring them closer together instead of setting them farther apart.

At the very same time there are many people, both young and old, who are rediscovering the consolations of religion. One of my students who was once Wiccan and then Presbyterian is now studying for confirmation in the Roman Catholic Church. Another who was raised Southern Baptist has become Russian Orthodox, while others have begun leaving their home churches in order to join The Rock, a nondenominational Christian movement that is planting churches all over northeast Georgia. As different as their destinations are, these converts are all drawn by a particular vision of the truth that strikes them as superior to others they have known.

While the dangers at either end of this scale are apparent—a vague universalism on one end and an airtight exclusivism on the other—the real danger, it seems to me, is losing the divine paradox that is built into biblical faith, namely, that the way to the universal God leads through a particular community of faith, whose teachings direct the faithful to recognize God's image in those outside the faith. I have Rabbi Jonathan Sacks to thank for the reminder that while Torah contains one verse commanding love of neighbor, it contains thirty-six verses commanding love of the stranger.[2] Jesus embodies these teachings in his encounters with Samaritans, Romans, and Canaanites, to whom he ministers with no requirement that they follow him, and when he dies, he dies for love not of some, but of all.

In both testaments, God's people are chosen to become blessings on all people, so that their religious identity becomes inseparable from how they treat those who do not share their religion (as well as those who do). While there is room for lively debate about what makes Christians different from anyone else, my nominee is *sacrificial love*, not only the kind that we see on the cross, but also the kind that is available to us every day, as we surrender all the things that guarantee our safety, our security, our rightness—up to and including the imperious aspects of our religion—in order to love our neighbors as ourselves.

Because I am aware of the difficulties such language poses for those whose sacrifices are not only assumed but required by the dominant cultures in which they live, let me add that I am thinking of sacrificial love at the corporate and not the individual level. While it is natural, in times like these, to preach in ways that will build up the church—by suggesting that only those inside of it see things aright, for instance, or that God's goal is to bring the world into the church—an alternative (and I think equally faithful) reading of the gospel is that God's goal is to bring the church into the world—to place the followers of Jesus at the service of all God's other children, until love has time to remake all their hearts. In this vision, the rewards of faith are not safety or security, but the promise of alarming and sometimes painful transformation.

If I drew the vision for you, then it would look like a bunch of concentric circles with God at the center instead of the church. Circling that center are ever-expanding rings of relationship that draw those who love God from inward-facing concerns to outward-facing ones. God's love for individuals opens into God's love for neighbors. God's love for neighbors opens into God's love for strangers. God's love for strangers opens into God's love for all creation, and God's love for all creation opens into the boundless cosmos of divine compassion, so that the reality at the center of the circle is the same reality in which the whole circle abides. In this spacious context, the church is found in the arrows that lead from each ring of relationship to the next, as those who love God strive to keep up with the expanding fullness of God's love.

Repeating "love" that many times in one paragraph makes me fear my own simplemindedness, but what I fear even more is the suspicion and enmity that I see building up between people of differing faiths. In many cases, the differences are between different kinds of Christians, but they are also between Christians and Jews, Jews and Muslims, Muslims and Hindus, Hindus and Christians. Conflicts between these communities would be dangerous enough if they were based only on clashes of culture or disputes over land, but once they are couched in terms of who is right about God, then they become deadly in a different kind of way. When those made in God's image hate or kill one another in God's name, then surely part of God dies with them.

Meanwhile, there are still Christians in this world who believe that how we treat one another is more important than how we express our beliefs. There are even some outside our faith who count on us to act on that. Last fall I shared a meal with a Muslim woman who was despondent over the headlines from Israel/Palestine. Suicide bombings were at a high, the road to peace was in ruins and those on both sides of the conflict had run out of words. "Jews and Muslims cannot hear each other anymore," she said. "It is up to the Christians now." When I put down my fork and stared at her, she said, "You are the peacemakers, are you not?"

What is the matter with preaching today? Perhaps it is that the life-and-death questions we wrestle with are too small—too self-interested—to draw much support from the living God. While we fuss over our church budgets and the salvation of our own souls, God is in the labor and delivery room with a world in travail, wondering where all the help has gone. Eloquence and learning are optional at this point. What God needs are human beings willing to give themselves full-time to the dangerous practice of love—making peace, saving lives, defending the defenseless, redistributing wealth—delivering the goods, Fosdick says, with the same single-mindedness as a cobbler delivering shoes.

Needless to say, preachers may give up any fantasies of success that they harbor in this regard. To preach the gospel is to duck rocks more often than you receive bouquets, but none of us is excused. Our consolation prize, as preachers, is that even when we miss the mark with our listeners, that does not mean our listeners miss the gospel. Even before they have shaken our hands at the door of the church and headed to their cars, they have begun thinking about the gospel that they did not hear from us. They have begun filling in what we left out, lingering long enough on something we said to clarify what they would have said in our place. They may even engage others in conversation about the gospel they did not hear, and while this knowledge does nothing to shore up our personal sense of success, we may still count it as gain instead of loss. It is our proof that God works around our words as well as through them, and that whatever is the matter with preaching today is not the first, last, or only thing that is the matter but simply the most recent.

As noble as our dreams of perfection may seem to us, they get in our way—not only because they keep us from risking failure, but also because they shine too much light on us. All things considered, the proclamation of the gospel has never depended on the golden tongues of great preachers, but on the beating wings of the Holy Spirit who—praise God!—continues to move over the face of the deep and bring the Word to life.

Notes

1. Anyone who loves Mary Oliver's poetry as much as I do recognizes this language from the last line of her poem, "The Summer Day," found in *New and Selected Poems* (Boston: Beacon, 1993), 94.
2. Jonathan Sacks, *The Dignity of Difference: How to Avoid the Clash of Civilizations* (New York: Continuum, 2002), 58.